Self-Publishing for Independent Authors

(A Beginner's Guide)

3rd Edition

Ian Hooper

Copyright © Ian Hooper, 2022
Published: 2022 by The Book Reality Experience
Leschenault, Western Australia

ISBN: 978-1-922670-66-3 - **Paperback 3rd Edition**
ISBN: 978-1-922670-82-3 - **eBook 3rd Edition**

All rights reserved.

The right of Ian Hooper to be identified as author of this Work has been asserted by him in accordance with sections 77 and 78 of the Copyright, Designs and Patents Act 1988.

Limit of liability / Disclaimer of Warranty: The Publisher and the author make no representations or warranties with respect to the accuracy or completeness of the contents of this work and specifically disclaim all warranties, including without limitation warranties of fitness for particular purpose. No warranty may be created or extended by sales or promotional materials. The advice and strategies contained herein may not be suitable for every occasion or situation. This work is sold with the understanding that the publisher is not engaged in rendering taxation, legal or other professional advice or services. If professional assistance is required, the services of a competent professional person should be sought. Neither the Publisher nor the author shall be liable for damages arising herefrom. The fact that an individual, organisation, or website is referred to in this work as a citation and/or potential source of further information does not mean that the author or the Publisher endorses the information, individual, organisation, or website or recommendations they/it make. Further, readers should be aware that Internet websites listed in this work may have changed or disappeared between when this work was written and when it is read.

No part of this publication may be reproduced, stored in a retrieval system, copied in any form or by any means, electronic, mechanical, photocopying, recording or otherwise transmitted without written permission from the publisher. You must not circulate this book in any format.

Cover Design by Brittany Wilson | Brittwilsonart.com

Dedication

To all the
Book Reality Authors
and
Book Reality Academy Students

Remember, as Dory didn't say,
"Just Keep Writing"

And for Christopher and Arthur
May you be writing on clouds

Also by Ian Andrew

The Wright & Tran Novels
Face Value
Flight Path
Fall Guys

Other Titles
A Time To Every Purpose

As Ian Hooper
The Little Book Of Silly Rhymes & Odd Verses
Slaughtered Nursery Rhymes: For Grown-Ups

Write till your ink be dry, and with your tears
Moist it again, and frame some feeling line
That may discover such integrity.

Act III, Scene II
The Two Gentlemen of Verona

Table of Contents

Foreword to the 3rd Edition i

1 - SO, YOU WANT TO BE A WRITER? 3

2 - THE INDIE AUTHOR 8

3 - WAYS AND MEANS 13

Kindle Direct Publishing.. *15*
Draft2Digital... *19*
IngramSpark.. *21*
Findaway Voices.. *22*

4 - KINDLE DIRECT PUBLISHING 24

Author/Publisher Information *26*
Payment & Banking.. *26*
Tax Information *29*
Uploading your Manuscript and Cover as an eBook *30*
ISBNs and ASINs... *38*
Kindle eBook Pricing... *40*
Kindle Reports.. *42*

5 - DRAFT2DIGITAL AGGREGATOR SERVICE 43

Edit Book – Details.. *46*
Edit Book – Layout.. *47*
Edit Book – Preview.. *48*
Edit Book – Publish... *49*
D2D Reporting.. *50*

6 - TRIM SIZE 52

Cover Template... *54*

7 - AMAZON'S KDP FOR PAPERBACK 56

Start Your New Project 57
Manuscript 59
Book Cover 59
Territories 62
Distribution and Pricing 62
Complete Setup 63
Publishing on KDP 64
Ordering Author Copies 64
Royalty Reports 65
Revisions 65

8 - INGRAMSPARK 67

Ingram Dashboard 71
Step 1 - Add New Title 72
Step 2 - Add New Title 73
Step 3 - Add New Title 79
The Alliance of Independent Authors 80
Help 81
Reports 81
Ordering Books 82
Approving the Proof 83

9 - FORMATTING FOR PRINT AND EBOOK 85

First - Learn to view your document correctly 87
Trim Size - Again 87
Section Breaks 89
Master your Headers and Footers. 90
Chapter Headings and Scene Breaks 91
Styles 92
Using the Built-In Heading Styles 94
Insert your own Hyperlinks 96
Insert a Hyperlinked Table of Contents. 96
Save your document as a PDF-A 97

10 - USING CALIBRE TO MAKE YOUR EPUB **100**

11 - AUDIO BOOKS **103**

    AMAZON'S VERY OWN, ACX *104*
    VOICE TALENT *107*
    PREPARATION *108*
    PUBLISHING AUDIO BOOKS *109*

12 - OTHER CONSIDERATIONS **112**

    LEGAL DEPOSIT *112*
    SELLING INTO BOOKSTORES *114*
    MARKETING *118*
    SOCIAL MEDIA *118*
    WEBSITES AND BLOGS AND COMPETITIONS *120*
    AMAZON'S AUTHOR CENTRAL & A+ CONTENT *121*
    EXPERT MARKETING COURSES AND FREEBIES *121*
    EBOOK MARKETING MEGA MAILING LISTS *122*
    READER REVIEWS *124*
    FESTIVALS *124*
    THE BOTTOM LINE *125*

ACKNOWLEDGEMENTS **129**

ABOUT THE AUTHOR **130**

ABSOLUTELY SHAMELESS ADVERTISING OPPORTUNITY **131**

INDEX **135**

Foreword to the 3rd Edition

In the four years since I first wrote this small guide, so many things have altered in the world of Print-on-Demand (PoD) publishing.

Createspace has been subsumed into the ever expanding KDP, Smashwords is part of Draft2Digital, and whilst those two 'mergers and/ or acquisitions' might look as if the PoD playing field is thinning out, in fact the opposite is true. More and more PoD providers are popping up left, right and centre. Meanwhile, traditional publishers, already thin on the ground, are (as I write) in the midst of a battle to merge two of America's biggest, (Penguin Random House and Simon & Schuster) to form a mammoth enterprise. Last I read of it, Stephen King is not happy. Now, I am a HUGE admirer of Stephen King, but personally, if I'm being honest, I care not a jot about the merger of traditional publishers. They are irrelevant to the Independent Author scene. And what a scene *it* is.

According to multiple reports from an array of agencies, the biggest growth sector in publishing is self-publishing and this covers all formats: print, e-book and audio. The latter format, although accessible to self-published authors, is not a walk in the park, but we'll get into those issues later.

Likewise, despite the growth of the sector, despite some self-published authors selling tens of thousands of books, despite some seeing their work turned into movies or a series on Netflix, despite more awards and mainstream associations opening their doors to allow 'us' in, some of the basics are still being missed.

Independent authors, indies, indys or self-publishing authors, whatever we might like to refer to ourselves as, have a responsibility to the wider 'indie'-community and of course, to the 'Dear Reader' who we want to buy our books.

We owe it to each other to represent in a way that does not cause traditional publishers, or mainstream media, to sigh and moan about us, but causes them to sigh that they didn't have the good sense to spot our talent earlier.

That means apart from writing a 'good' story (an entirely subjective grading, which is why it will not be discussed any further in this little book. I mean... a *good* story for one is drivel for another!) – we MUST look to editing, interior formatting, cover design and basic marketing as essentials, not *nice to haves*. And we must get over any sense of entitlement that we should be *allowed in* or *respected*, or treated by the book industry in a way we might consider, *fair*. This is business and fair is a reading on a barometer.

We have to control what we can and not worry about what we can't. We have to be thick-skinned against the reviewers who dislike us and passionately enthusiastic for those readers who love us. We have to be independently-minded, self-focussed, self-believing and self-starting. We have to take control of our own *book-fate* and manage it from first draft to final proof, for if we do all of that, then we can confidently self-publish as an independent author.

My hope is that this little book, updated to reflect the current state of self-publishing, helps you in your journey.

Ian Hooper
Western Australia
September 2022

1

So, You Want to Be a Writer?

Congratulations. On the simple assumption that you do actually write things down, be that poems or 'flash fiction', short stories or full novels, then you're already a 'Writer'. There is no mystery in the way this works. You write, you're a writer. But I guess, like most, you were thinking more of your books being traditionally published, adorning the front window of your local bookshop, people queuing at barricaded doors, the clock ticking towards midnight, hordes breaking through to purchase many millions of your latest offering to the world?

Yeah, let's be honest, that's unlikely to happen.

Not that it couldn't and it is always worth hanging on to the dream, but you have to be aware of the realities and the reality is there is one Ms Rowling in a generation, or perhaps even two or three generations, so let's not be holding our breath. Saying that, even the simple fact of getting your book published in a traditional way, by the likes of Penguin Random House, or Hachette or any of the other 'Biggies' is worth hanging onto. It really is, for the big 'Elephant in the Independent Publishing Room' that has to be dealt with first and foremost, is that traditional publishing still holds all the advantages when it comes to their 'big-name' authors. The 'Trads' will throw money and industry insider-information at the problem of getting sales. They will advertise in airports from Australia to Zambia, on busses, in newspapers, online, offline, in social media, on tube-trains in London and anywhere else you can think of. They will fly their new and valued authors to book fairs and festivals, book launches and media spots, they will assign marketing people and publicists. You will be lorded like the writing genius you are.

Well… Perhaps.

If you are a massive best seller then yes, but if you aren't then all of that marketing falls by the wayside pretty quick. If you're not in the top dozen or so names on a Trad's portfolio, then a lot of that marketing and publicity is going to drop back on to you. Yet, even with that being the case, the Trads still hold the trump cards when it comes to distribution, market penetration and market visibility. They have deep pockets and it is the way it is. At present. It might change in the future, but don't be shocked if it doesn't. They have money invested in the game. It is in their best interests to keep it loaded in their favour.

Many bookstores and many mainstream media reviewers still sneer at the non-traditionally published author. Most will not entertain them. So, if you want to be a writer, my suggestion is that you send your manuscript to every agent under the sun and then to every publisher under it too. If you get picked up as the next hot thing, then you have well and truly made it. If you don't, well let's not despair. For that is where, despite all that traditional publishing might wish, the game has changed.

At the start of the 21st Century there were realistically only two ways to get published. The traditional method as already described and the vanity method. Vanity publishing was where you went to a printer with your manuscript and cover art, paid them an amount of money to print your book and took the copies home. The print run, to be commercially viable, had to be significant, often in the thousands of copies for a commensurate amount of money paid to the printing company.

It was a perfectly sound idea and the likes of Beatrix Potter did just that to see her books published, but the main issue with it was getting the books sold.

Short of walking around each and every bookshop in your locale in the hope that they would take some copies, there was little opportunity for the vanity published author to sell their works to readers. If you were lucky enough to live in a major city then you had more bookshops to visit, but even then there would be limited uptake. Invariably, after your friends and family had received their allotted copies, the loft of your house benefitted from an extra layer of insulation.

Like I said, at the start of the 2000s this two-pronged approach to publishing, Trad or Vanity, changed. A new kid came on the block. Slowly at first, with limited resources and capability, the advent of commercially viable Print on Demand technologies allowed any writer to not only self-publish their book, but have it distributed to a global audience through online sellers. In 2007, when Amazon brought out their Kindle reading devices for electronic books and complimented it with their Kindle Direct Publishing arm, the world of the self-published author exploded. Literally, it was like the big bang. Millions of new titles have been published each and every year since then and the number keeps growing. Yet it wasn't just about the number of books being published. There was another quantum change. No longer would the gate-keepers of the traditional publishing companies dictate who should and shouldn't be published. No more would the limited reach of the vanity presses stifle an author's ambitions. No! Now was the new wave. Now artistic expression would flow unfettered... Now imagine Mel Gibson in a kilt shouting freedom at the top of his lungs,

"Freedom for authors…"

Yeah… not so much… Sadly the revolution didn't quite transpire the way we might have wished for. What actually happened was a whole tsunami of terrible writing swamped the market. Bypassing the traditional gatekeepers of publishing did indeed mean anyone could publish and with absolutely no standards to meet that is what happened. Anyone could publish. Whether they could actually conjugate a verb or not. Heck, whether they could spell 'verb' or not.

With the dross came an inevitable consequence. The stigma of the self-published author was well and truly reinforced and the amount of poor writing that washed across the average reader was nearly enough to kill the whole idea.

But not quite.

For some self-published authors determined that if they were going to try and compete with the 'Trad' way, then they had to up their game. They had to get their covers designed professionally. They had to get their work edited professionally. They had to step up their knowledge of distribution methods and marketing. They had to enhance their public profiles. Most stumbled their way along, learning through trial and error for there was no font of knowledge to visit. There was no university course to take, no 'Idiots Guide' to read. Separately at first, then in small informal groups and later in more formal associations, their publishing skillsets began to come together.

Most of this new breed of authors incrementally improved their overall product and each book they brought out was held to a higher standard than the last. Soon it became apparent that this new breed of self-published author was managing the same processes that a Traditional publishing house did. On occasion they would even be able to sub-contract the self-same editors and illustrators that worked for the Trad houses.

The only difference was the self-published author managed it all themselves. They had transitioned from self-published to independently published.

The era of the Indie Author had arrived.

2

The Indie Author

Queue fireworks and banners? Indie authors rock the world of publishing and dominate sales figures? Well, actually, yes. By volume of sales, independently published authors outweigh all the Traditional publishing houses combined. However, in a quirk of economics, the Trads still have the advantage on actual monetary amounts. That's not hard to understand. If you release a Kindle copy of your book you will probably have to pitch it at 3.99 dollars, pounds or euros depending on your marketplace. Trads with big name authors can charge a lot more and the thousands and thousands of followers for that particular headline author will pay that higher recommended retail price. Indies are therefore making a much smaller income. Worse still, the average Indie author with modest sales across all formats, electronic (eBooks), print (paperbacks and hardbacks) and audio, will make less than US$10,000 per year.

"Ugh! So what's the point?" I hear you mumble, as tears of reality-infused disappointment soak down your face, dropping to sizzle in your soon-to-be-discarded keyboard. The point is, you might be the exception. The point is your writing may be the one to capture the interest of thousands and you end up being that rarest of beasts, the internationally acknowledged Indie. The point is, actually, none of that matters.

The only thing that matters is this. If you, like thousands of other writers each and every month, get rejected by a Traditional publishing house then Indie publishing offers you a realistic alternative. A way to see your book released into the world where it might be read by one… or one million readers. The scale isn't important. The fact somebody is reading your book is. You will be a published writer and no one can stop you. Oh, I suppose there is another thing that matters. Those rejections will put you in some mighty fine writing company. Google, 'Famous authors rejected'. No, seriously, go on, Google it now, I'll wait… (But don't get distracted and spend hours looking at cats).

§

See? King, Plath, Kipling, Christie, Hemmingway, Orwell, Heller, ROWLING. All turned down multiple times by a wide range of companies. I think my favourite example, although terribly sad, is Herman Melville of *Moby Dick* fame. Now his is a case worth considering. Turned down time and time again and given the most ludicrous suggestions for how it could be made more commercial. Thankfully he ignored them and eventually published under a system we would call 'Hybrid Publishing' nowadays. He met some of the costs himself and the publishing company did the rest, releasing the novel in 1851. Even then *Moby Dick* didn't become an instant bestseller. In fact it sold 'modestly' and that's an understatement. According to a critical text of the book published in 1988[1], *Moby-Dick* was out of print during the last four years of Melville's life, having sold 2,300 in its first eighteen months of release and on average 27 copies a year for the next

---

[1] Melville, H. *Moby-Dick, or The Whale.* Northwestern-Newberry Edition of the Writings of Herman Melville 6. Evanston, Ill.: Northwestern U. Press, 1988 Editor Tanselle

34 years, equalling 3,215 copies. Herman's earnings from the book added up to a grand total of $1,260.

He died in 1891 and it wasn't until the 1920's, when a number of reviewers looked again at the story, that the 'ball of interest' began to gather pace. Eventually the momentum grew and the book's fame was guaranteed. Nowadays acknowledged as one of the all-time great American novels, it regularly appears in *top ten* lists like the Guardian's 'Greatest Novels of all Time'[2] and its opening line, 'Call me Ishmael' was voted the best opening line ever by the American Book Review. Not bad for a book where the author had to self-fund part of its production.

The other example you should probably hang on to in times of gloom and doom and despondency, when you are wondering if your writing is any good at all, is Dickens and *A Christmas Carol*.

Although previously successful with the likes of *Oliver Twist*, due to a disagreement with his former publisher over more recent commercial failures, Dickens arranged to pay for the publishing of *A Christmas Carol* himself, in exchange for a bigger percentage of the profits. Despite selling very well in the first year, he didn't make as much as he reckoned he would, but this was mostly because of the very high production costs involved with coloured endpapers and gilt-edging to the pages. Bear that in mind, he made it too fancy. Although he did do alright with it in the end. In fact, it has never been out of print since first being published and I've lost count of the number of film, stage or TV adaptations that have been made. I wonder what his publisher, who rejected it, would think?

With these two examples in mind then, it is worth remembering, the Indie author process is not for those who can't get

---

[2] www.theguardian.com/books/2014/jan/13/100-best-novels-observer-moby-dick

published by Traditional publishing houses because they are not *good* enough. It is for those that are not *lucky* enough. That's all.

It is for those who do not want to spend the next two, five, ten years hoping that their manuscript gets seen by the right person in the right mood on the right day. A person who will eventually say, "Oh, I think we should take a chance on this." And even if they do say that, here's a point to ponder regarding the chance they might take.

The first edition of *Harry Potter and the Philosopher's Stone* ran to only 500 hardback copies. That's it. That's how much of a chance they were prepared to take on a book that went on to sell 120 million (and counting) copies. See? Trad publishers are not infallible judges of writing talent or potential.

Oh and Trad also make mistakes inside their books. That first Harry Potter had a repetition of '1 wand' on Harry's school supplies shopping list. It's on page 53 and if your copy has it, well done, it's worth a lot of money.

Having established that the Indie path is not a back alley to publishing for the failed author, but a bright boulevard of opportunity for the entrepreneurial author, I suppose we should explain how you actually do it. But first, some advice. None of the following tips and techniques are going to be of any use to you whatsoever if you haven't done something quite important first. And what is that?

Written your book

Yeah, that's the most important thing. Write and finish your book. Be that a poem anthology or a collection of short stories or the next great novel for the 21st century, you actually have to write it. Finish it. Re-work it and re-draft it and personally edit it and edit it again, then pass it to an external editor and edit it and edit it again and and and… and yes, it is that obvious and that simple but you'd be amazed at the number of want-to-be writers who haven't actually written anything. So don't be them. Be you and finish your book. Once you have, or at least once you are a long way towards that goal, then you can think about moving on to Chapter 3 and exploring who you will use to publish your manuscript.

3

Ways and Means

The rest of this book is going to look at electronic books (eBooks), old-fashioned book-books (print) and audio books (audio).

Within eBook and print books there are a number of formats that you can publish in. You'll be familiar with paperback or hardback, but what about ePublication format or Mobi format?[3] Then there is the page size, page weight, cover finish and a myriad of other options. All in all it adds up to a lot of choices for your one book. However, some Indies elect not to bother with physical print books and only use eBooks. Some Indies want print books, but not for distribution into bookshops. Some Indies want all of it, including an audio version. Regardless of all other decisions, it is extremely likely that as a minimum you will want to release your work as an eBook.

For Indie authors there is no question that the world of eBooks offers an amazing opportunity. A simple interface for the purchase of books worldwide is provided by the likes of Amazon, Apple, Kobo, Barnes & Noble and many more. There is no

---

[3] Note that as of 2021 Amazon does not 'ingest' Mobi format and by end 2022 the Mobi format will likely disappear altogether.

requirement to warehouse stock and the ability to change or amend manuscripts is swift, as is the setting of prices. Add to this the incredible reach of aggregator services like Draft2Digital that save you the hassle of having to distribute to each and every sales outlet separately and the world of eBooks for Indie authors is relatively cheap to enter and very easy to manage.

I say relatively cheap as you must remember that to be taken seriously as an Indie author you need to have an editor for the interior of your book and a designer for the cover. Of course, if you know one of each and they owe you a favour, then that's great. If you don't then the costs can vary widely. The experience and standing in the industry of the editor or artist will dictate what they charge and what you can afford will dictate what you pay. But you need to be aware that you're likely to be paying something. In fact, you should be paying something because you need professionals on your 'team'. My company, *The Book Reality Experience*, has a number of editors and designers that assist Indie authors, so if you are stuck, look us up.

Once you have the editing and the cover done to your satisfaction and your book is 'good to go' then how do you actually get it into the world? Well, as you may suspect, there are multiple providers and suppliers of PoD services. It would be impossible to mention them all, let alone cover how to access and use each one, so the rest of this book is going to concentrate on five pathways, using four main companies. They haven't been picked out for any reason other than after my own trials and errors these are the main ones I use. To be clear then, there are other ways and other companies offering similar services, these are simply my preferences and of course, a lot of what I will expand on will carry across to most providers.

Why did I choose these providers? Because they allow me to do all that I wish to with reasonably easy interfaces and with minimal effort. Subsequently I have gone on to work with some of them more closely and have developed good working relationships with them, but at the outset I simply gave them a try and discovered that I liked them. There is one other provider that I use, BookVault, but they don't feature in here at present. Maybe the 4th edition of this guide will expand to include them. For now though, let's deal with my current *Fab Four*.

For the direct supply of eBooks and print to Amazon, I use Amazon's dedicated Kindle Direct Publishing (KDP). I supplement that with the aggregator Draft2Digital to supply eBooks on a wide distribution model to a range of other outlets. For wide print distribution I use IngramSpark for supplying other online retailers as well as distribution to physical, 'bricks-and-mortar' bookshops. IngramSpark also handle the production and distribution of some books that Amazon's KDP can't produce, or where Amazon's pricing is not competitive. Finally, I use Findaway Voices to handle the distribution of my audio books. We'll look at each one of these in detail in later chapters, but for now, a quick introduction.

Kindle Direct Publishing

Kindle Direct Publishing (KDP) produces eBooks and print books. For ease, I'll deal with each separately.

KDP started out as Amazon's own eBook publishing interface producing Kindle format books for sale exclusively within Amazon's global online stores. Founded in November 2007, it changed the face of eBook publishing and due to the various features available through its interface I elected to have an account directly with them. For all other eBook retailers I use an aggregator service, but more about that later.

The great news about KDP is that it is free to use. The other great news is the royalty returns. For eBooks and depending on the price point you choose, you can get up to 70% royalties. That price does have to be between $2.99 and $9.99 US, but most Indies set their books at $3.99 or $4.99, so that's okay. You may think, that's not a lot for all the hard work and effort that goes into writing a novel, but I suppose, were you to sell 100,000 copies and get 70% of $3.99 per copy, (there is a small deduction for transmission of the book title over the network)… you'd end up with about $279,000 and you'd probably cope.

KDP also allows you to enrol your eBook into Amazon's KDP Select program. Readers who are members of the Kindle Unlimited Program can download and read your book for 'free'. Of course they have paid a monthly membership so it isn't really free. You as the author get a percentage payout of the Kindle Unlimited fund for that month based on how many downloads and, crucially, how many actual pages of your book were read. Yes. They can track that on the Kindle reading devices. For those top selling or top 'borrowed' authors there are bonus payments given at the end of each month.

Overall, the KDP eBook interface is simple to use, the sales reports available are comprehensive and easy to manage and the royalty rates are extremely good. Mainly though, the attraction of the Amazon Kindle store is that it has the vast majority of eBooks sales worldwide and especially within the big five English-speaking marketplaces. According to the Author Earnings Report (2017)[4] Amazon enjoyed 83% of all eBook sales across the US, UK, Canada, Australia and New Zealand. Whilst that market share has reportedly dropped to something in the region of 67% for 2020 figures, it is still leading the market by a landslide.

In short, Amazon's Kindle format is a 'must have' if you want your books out in the eBook marketplace. As is using KDP if

---

[4] http://authorearnings.com/report/february-2017/

you want a seamless and hassle-free way to get your print book into Amazon 'stores'.

Initially KDP only published Kindle eBooks while paperbacks were produced within CreateSpace, who had been acquired by Amazon in 2005. In 2018, following a few months of a Beta paperback program roll-out, KDP replaced Createspace entirely. At time of writing (September 2022) KDP is also rolling out a Beta hardback program and I would predict that this will go fully live before the end of 2022, if not sooner.

For paperback and hardback the royalty rate is 60%, but you do have to pay printing costs. As an example, for a paperback of 260 pages, priced at $11.95 US dollars, you would receive $3.22 in royalties per sale. Again, seems modest, but you are not having to arrange a print run or warehousing or anything else. Someone you may or may not know buys your book on Amazon and you get $3.22 (90 days later, but you still get it).

The interface for print books is equally easy to use and it has a superb viewing mechanism to inspect your book layout and format. Once again, it is free and any amendments or changes that you make and upload are also free of charge.

Now, a few things. Firstly, using KDP means that your book (or any amendments to your book) will get pushed through to Amazon stores very quickly indeed. This is great as it means that minor, post-publication edits to your book can be made and uploaded within hours. What do I mean by post-publication edits? Well, let's say you spot a *speelink mistook* after you have published – (it happens, don't be so hard on yourself) – anyway, it can be addressed and made 'right' and any customer buying your book from then on will get the corrected copy.

The KDP interface also allows changes to the recommended retail price at any time and that is a definite advantage over some external services that limit price changes to once a week.

KDP will also provide what they call 'expanded distribution' for print books, where they will make your book available to bricks-and-mortar bookshops and online retailers. They will further distribute your book to academic institutions and libraries, but these last two are only if you have used one of their International Standard Book Numbers (ISBNs). What's one of those? You know the funny number with a barcode you see on all printed books? That's an ISBN. Anyway, we shall discuss those in depth later, but suffice to say at the moment, this expanded distribution is problematic.

You see KDP is owned by Amazon and they are the biggest seller of books in the world. So for another bookseller to have to order stock from them is a bit like a car mechanic having to order their spare parts from another mechanic's shop, instead of a centralised parts dealer. Or for a restaurant having to buy their ingredients from another restaurant rather than the wholesale supplier. It makes no economic sense as you are paying your biggest competitor to supply your stock. Therefore, it is recommended that you don't use Amazon's expanded distribution if you want to attempt to get your books into physical stores. I say attempt as it is far from easy whatever supplier you use, but in my experience the best option to manage the difficult task is to use IngramSpark.

We shall explore what makes them a great alternative a little later, but before we leave KDP, I want to tell you why, despite the fact you aren't going to use them for expanded distribution, you should have an account with them.

The simple truth is that KDP's interface is a doddle to work with, their digital proofing system is a venerable work of art and all uploads and changes made to your manuscript and cover are processed free of charge. That means you can upload as many times as you like and 'see' your book laid out in the manner it will appear when printed.

Now stop for a moment!! I'll say it here and I will repeat it later. If this is the first time you are printing your book, you will **NEED TO** order a proper proof copy as the physical world occasionally surprises in comparison to a digital rendering on a screen, regardless of how good the system is. That said, for subsequent revisions and for the period before going to print, KDP's interface wins hands-down. To be completely honest, even if you decided you were going to manage all of your paperback distribution through an external supplier, I would still upload the manuscript to KDP, such is the convenience of their proofing system. If you do use them to publish, their reporting systems are excellent as well.

However, as I said, we don't want to use KDP print for trying to sell to others and KDP eBooks are Kindle only. So how do we get out to the rest of the world? That would mean an aggregator for eBooks and a wide distribution for print. For the former, I use Draft2Digital.

Draft2Digital

Draft2Digital do print books and eBooks and have a tie-in for audio books. I only use them for eBooks, but that's just my preference. Why do I use them at all? Well, each eBookseller, Amazon with Kindle, Apple with their iBooks, Kobo, Barnes & Noble and the plethora of others out there all have their own interfaces through which an Indie author can upload books. Each interface has its own quirks and foibles. Now, to digress a little…

Back in a former life I worked in a UK Military Electronic Warfare Unit. The military being the military, have a tendency to train you to quite a high level in whatever discipline they want you to work in, so for that particular role I was trained as a computer analyst and software programmer, exposed to multiple programming languages and every type of computer from mainframes to PCs. I was trained in languages that were designed for real-time applications through to the everyday Microsoft Office type of programs. I eventually, years later, ended up as an accredited Microsoft instructor. Why is any of this relevant? Well, only in so much that it hopefully illustrates I am quite well-versed in 'computer things'.

Despite this aptitude and experience, a number of the interfaces for a number of the online retailers of eBooks confused me to the point where I threw in the towel and gave up. Some were okay but others were diabolical in their fastidiousness and inability to do things easily. It became so annoying that for quite some time I only published through Amazon's KDP. Fast forward a year or so and I became aware of Draft2Digital (D2D). They are, according to their own website:

A publishing aggregator ... that lets you upload your manuscript in one place, and then distributes your work to multiple channels ... to get a high-quality, mutually beneficial experience..[5]

I have found the D2D interface incredibly easy to use and they have some nice 'add-ons' which we will look at later. Royalty rates are dictated by the sellers and D2D take a 15% net cut of the royalty coming to you. For the peace of mind and ease of service they offer, I feel it is well worth it. The other advantage is that I don't have to use them to distribute to Amazon as I already have that covered with my KDP account.

As I mentioned previously, there are lots of other aggregators out there, but for the purpose of this guide, I'll be using D2D.

---

[5] https://www.draft2digital.com/blog/is-an-aggregator-right-for-you/

IngramSpark

IngramSpark is owned by Lightning Source, a business unit of Ingram Content Group which is one of the largest distributors and wholesalers of books in the world. They are therefore one of the main places that booksellers go to buy their stock. In 2013 when IngramSpark was launched, it was primarily intended for small publishers, but has rapidly adapted to embrace the rise of the Indie author. In a real sense the Indie is of course the veritable epitome of the small publisher.

In addition to having the distribution sorted for other booksellers to buy your books, it also allows a modicum of flexibility with regard to the discounts you can apply (all booksellers will want to buy your book at a discounted price, obviously, as they need to be able to sell it for a profit). Further, IngramSpark has a printing outlet in Australia, which for any Indies based down here (like me) is a huge bonus when it comes to ordering proofs or stock for author events or festivals.

I should declare that a couple of years after beginning to use them I was invited on to their Independent Authors International Advisory Board, which was a great initiative and allowed us to put forward suggestions, but sadly that 'board' was wrapped up a few years ago. It is also important to note that for Ingram (and all the rest of the services I am recommending in here), I am not being paid to praise them. Whatever I write about their services is solely based on my experience of them. Also, some of Ingram's reporting interfaces are dire, their proofing model is not a patch on KDP, the overall interface is a bit clunky and if you are not a member of the Alliance of Independent Authors, their revision and upload charges can become quite hefty. All of that said, they have the independent distribution methods that you need if you are serious about getting your books into shops.

Again though, like the aggregator service for eBooks, there are numerous other PoD suppliers out there. Some, like Lulu, have been going for years, others are just coming in to the market. Go explore and discover what is out there for yourself. Which is what I did when I went looking for audio books.

Findaway Voices

D2D have a hook-up / tie-in with Findaway Voices, but when I thought about making an audio book, I went to the big player in the marketplace first: Amazon ACX.

They have actors looking to read books and if you go on there as an author looking for an actor, ACX will do the "matchmaking" and you can produce an audio book for nothing. Except you get nothing for nothing and so there are a few things to be aware of, like royalty rates and rights attribution and the length of those rights deals. Crucially for me, being in Australia meant I couldn't use them. ACX only operate in a few countries and unless I fancied pretending not to be in Australia, that was that for me.

As it happens, I think I had a lucky escape. At the same time as I was starting to consider recording audio books, the whole 'Audiblegate Scandal' broke. If you are not aware of Audiblegate, then try searching on the net for articles like this: *How Audible and ACX Betrayed Authors* or *Audiblegate Campaign: Fair Deal for Rights Holders*. Just don't do it now, you'll be there for hours. Suffice it to say that I decided, even if I could have used ACX, I preferred not to.

I went instead with what was then a relatively small start-up, Findaway Voices. Since then they have been acquired by Spotify – ah well, you never know what is around the corner.

Anyway, Findaway are easy to use, with a good interface and they distribute audio books to all the main outlets I wanted to use. We'll come on to what they are and how it all works later, but be aware **NOW** that audio book royalties are **A JOKE**. In my humble opinion, they are the worst return on investment I have ever come across. I paid out for narrators, studio technicians, as well as my own time and effort, all to release my fledgling book into the world and see it sell on a retail platform so that I could earn… wait for it… 26cents! Whereas the same book, on a different platform, for the same retail price, can make $6.00. The average is about $2.00 for a book where the retailer is making in excess of $15.00 per sale.

You might ask, why don't you just sell it on the one giving you $6? Good question. Because the first is Amazon's Audible platform which is, of course, the biggest seller of audio books in the world… I mean, I'd be depressed, but that's not what it's all about… is it? No! It's about having an audio version of my book out there, read by a professional (in my case, a former Game of Thrones actress) and being happy about it. And I am. Mostly. But you should be aware. So it doesn't surprise you later.

Right! Still with me?

Those are the four companies I use as my *ways and means* of getting my books into the world. Now's a good time to have a break and go and research those other things I mentioned, for when you get back, we'll take a closer look at each of the ways, beginning with Kindle Direct Publishing.

4

Kindle Direct Publishing

Kindle Direct Publishing (KDP) is Amazon's own publishing unit and allows authors to independently publish their books in print and eBooks. The latter are exclusively for Kindle readers and Kindle Apps. Some fundamentals to know:
- It is NOT necessary to own a Kindle device to download and read Kindle books. You can download an app on any device including PCs and Macs.
- It is not necessary to have a US Tax Number to register for KDP.
- It is not necessary to exclusively limit your eBook distribution to Amazon only.
- It is not necessary to restrict the price of your eBook to between 2.99 and 9.99 (US dollars).
- KDP interface is free for you to upload your book and cover to.
- KDP will instantly (almost) create a product page for you in Amazon's online stores.

I am sure there are lots of objections that lots of people could make about the global domination of Amazon, about their monopolies, about their... whatever... Personally I have a few concerns myself about their impact on the global book market, but... They are a phenomenal business who have become as big as they are by offering outstanding customer service and innovation. KDP was one such innovation.

To begin then, go to:

https://kdp.amazon.com/en_US/

You will be presented with a login screen that allows you to use your standard Amazon login (if you have one) or to register a new identity if you don't.

If necessary, follow the prompts for a new registration, including accepting the terms and conditions once you are happy with them, and then you will be presented with the KDP dashboard. It is a plain looking interface with four main tabs:

- Bookshelf (where your future titles will appear)
- Reports (where you will find details of your sales)
- Community (A huge archive of online help forums)
- Marketing (A suite of marketing tips and tools to assist you in getting word of your book out there).

Up at the very top of the screen are four smaller menu options:

- Your Account (Your profile, banking and tax information)
- Language selection (Self-explanatory)
- Help (A comprehensive archive of help articles)
- Sign Out (which does what you think and has two little emoji faces for you to give feedback on KDP).

You need to finish setting up your account, so either click on the link on the main screen that says **Update Now**, or click on *your account* in the top menu of the screen.

You are now looking at a screen that has three main components to it. Your Author/Publisher information (name, address, telephone number etc), Payment and Banking (how you get paid) and finally your tax information (the information the US Internal Revenue Service need).

Author/Publisher Information

You start by selecting individual or corporation. You may have registered a company to be your own publishing identity, or you may be just you, or the equivalent of a "Sole Trader" (Australian term for a one-person business). Select whichever you are, but note, I am only going to cover the steps required for an individual to register. The corporation is much the same, but the tax interview later is slightly different and requires more input, so we shan't be looking at that. If you are trying to register as a corporation, probably easier to email me if you have a specific question (ian@bookreality.com).

Okay, so assuming you have selected Individual, enter your date of birth (American date style, so month first), then your country or region and then your name, address and phone number. Now, this is your publisher name if you have one, or simply your full legal entity name. **Not your penname**, that will go into the record for any individual books you upload. It needs your actual name for now. The rest of the information is standard, but one little issue with the telephone number; if you want to put an international code in then you have to use the **+** rather than 00. So for a UK number you would put **+**44 and follow this with the rest of the number, minus the leading zero.

Payment & Banking

Potentially the most important information you will enter is where royalties due to you will be paid. Most of the information needed is straightforward, but you should be aware of a few little quirks and overall, how royalty payments are managed.

There are three ways that Amazon's KDP pay royalties:
- Direct Deposit, also known as Electronics Fund Transfer (EFT) paid into bank accounts that are registered in the US, Canada, UK, Europe, or in a limited fashion, Australia. This is the most convenient way to receive payments and EFT payments are not subject to a minimum threshold.
- Wire Transfer, a form of EFT but that has certain threshold requirements.
- Bank Cheque (check), yes the old fashioned bank cheque sent out in the mail. This too is subject to a threshold.

These threshold amounts are worth exploring. Each country that you sell to via their own particular Amazon store (.co.uk, .com, .com.au, .ca etc) will register their sales individually. That means if you sell an amount of books that earns you $90 of royalties in the US it is held separately from the £90 you may have made through sales in the UK. This is significant as each and every sales region has threshold amounts that must be met before royalties are paid out using wire transfer or cheque. The standard threshold is 100 of whichever currency is applicable.

Of course, if you have UK, US, Canadian or European accounts then you get paid via EFT and there is no minimum threshold. In Australia, your AUD sales are paid via EFT and the majority of others will be via wire transfer. Except Brazil, who still send their royalties out by cheque.

The easiest way to get paid quickly and without thresholds is to open a multi-national currency account. You do that by registering with the likes of **Wise**, a system that allows you US, UK, Australian, European and other currency accounts situated in the respective country. It is extremely low-cost, highly-efficient and will allow you to have payments made from any of the Print on Demand accounts, significantly bypassing the larger threshold amounts. There are other multi-currency accounts out there, but personally I cannot praise Wise highly enough. If you want to sign up for an account (and yes, you and I will both get an incentive for signing up) you can use this link:

https://wise.com/invite/u/johnh1722

Whatever payment method you select, cleared royalties (those over any minimum threshold) are paid according to the following KDP guidelines:

We pay royalties approximately 60 days following the end of the calendar month in which your royalties meet the payment threshold. You'll receive separate royalty payments for each Amazon store in which you have chosen to distribute your title.

You will be asked for a routing number, a BIC number or an IBAN number depending on the country your account is in:
- The routing number for Australian accounts is the BSB code. For UK accounts it is equivalent to the Sort Code.
- The BIC number or SWIFT code is an 8 or 11 character code that is bank specific. You can get it either via a Google search or (and safer) by giving your bank a ring and asking them.
- IBAN is usually required for UK held accounts and is the International Bank Account Number. For this you want to ring your bank directly and get it from them as it is account specific.

Once you have filled that all in, save it and move onto the tax interview.

Tax Information

In the early years of the Indie author, if you weren't a US citizen then the registration of your US tax information was, to say the least, cumbersome. It required you to gain tax registration numbers, be they individual or company, from the US Internal Revenue Service (IRS) and on some occasions attend your local US Embassy or Consulate and get an affidavit stamped. Now, all of that is a dim and distant memory as you can complete the full tax interview requirements online in a matter of minutes.

Within KDP you click on the 'Complete Tax Information' button and work your way through the interview questions. I urge you to take your time as this is a legal document required by the IRS and so you want to make sure you fill it in correctly. Most of the information asked for is straightforward but some things can be a little confusing.

It begins with a fairly simple set of questions and the main one is 'Are you are a US citizen for tax purposes?' If yes, then the rest of the form is straightforward and will use your existing Social Security Number or Individual Tax Identification Number. If you are not a US citizen then the form will require a bit more detail. Again, the questions are relatively straightforward, but on the assumption you are not acting as an intermediary, you will be prompted to affirm a series of statements and then enter a tax identification number. For most people who are not US citizens you can now select that you have a foreign (non-U.S.) ID number.

If you are a UK resident for tax purposes, that will be your National Insurance Number. If Australian, it will be your Tax File Number. If you are any other nationality it will be whatever tax identification number you use within your own country's tax system. But why do you have to register at all?

The reason for doing this is that Amazon will withhold 30%

of any royalty due to you unless you are in a nation with a tax agreement with the USA. So, for example, Australia has an agreement whereby if you provide an Australian tax ID then Amazon will only withhold 5% of your royalty for tax purposes. This is obviously a good thing when compared to 30% being withheld.

The last thing that will make all of this very quick is if you select to have the resultant Form 1042-S delivered electronically. That allows you to tick a number of legally binding statements and then 'sign' the document electronically. Once that is done the tax interview and forms will be lodged automatically for you by Amazon.

Having completed these account requirements you can upload your manuscript. Before you do that though, your manuscript needs to be formatted appropriately to sail through the Amazon requirements. That formatting will be covered in a later chapter, but for now we will assume you have a completed manuscript and cover.

I am also going to assume you want to make a paperback and an eBook version of your book. The good news is that if you do want to make both, then realistically you only have to enter the details once. So let's begin. Go to the Bookshelf 'tab' on the main KDP screen. From there, click the large yellow button **"+Create"**.

This will ask you what you want to create, Kindle eBook, paperback, hardback or a series.

Let's begin with a Kindle eBook. click on **"Create eBook"**.

Uploading your Manuscript and Cover as an eBook

You now have three screens of information to fill in. But fear not, the beauty about the KDP upload interface is that there are common-sense explanations given for each input and you will already know most of the information being asked for, such as the title of your book, any subtitles you were planning on using, etc. However, some of the requirements can be a little counter-intuitive.

Select the language of your book. Note that there are quite comprehensive lists under the dropdown, including Arabic and other languages that would flow right to left instead of the 'western' left to right. I have helped an author make a paperback and eBook in Farsi and Arabic. It is doable, but it is fiddly. We shan't be dealing with it in here. Again, if this is something you need help with, contact us directly.

Put in your **Title** (make sure you spell it properly!!) and the **sub-title**, if any. Then there is a part that asks is this a series. If it is, click on **add series detail**. It will open a separate box, click on **create series** (subsequently with other books you will click on Existing Series) then nominate this book as **main content**.

You then click on **Go to series setup**. This will open a whole new screen. Choose your language again. Enter the Series Title (And have a good think about that first. Perhaps Google a few to make sure it is fairly unique, try and make it relevant, or make it simple).

Then choose if it is an ordered series (books 1, 2 and 3 etc) or just a collection that is unordered but "belong together"… and if ordered, which book number this one. Enter a series description. Note, this is not the book's description, this is broader. Hopefully the examples on the following page will help:

We have a children's illustrated book called, *Janey Just in Case*. It is book 1 in a series and has a book description of:

> *Tomorrow is Janey's first day of school and worries are falling heavily on her shoulders...*
>
> Waking early, she fills her back pack adding a few extra's... just in case!
>
> *After all, you never know what you might need for your first day of school...*

The series itself is called **The Janey Series** and the overall series description is:

> *A series of books aimed at new school (primary) students, that explore social themes of new experiences, including excitement, nerves, anxiety, sharing, caring, bullying and the importance of kindness, friendship and teamwork.*

We also have a series of crime thrillers. They have titles like Face Value, Flight Path and Fall Guys. The series is called after the two main characters: Wright & Tran and so it is: **A Wright & Tran Novel** – which might sound weird, but when displayed on screen in the Amazon "shop" it looks like this:

Face Value: A Wright & Tran Novel

The series description is:

> *Two women, veterans of the United Kingdom's armed forces, now scrape a living as Private Investigators. Until they acquire a new client who offers a lot more in the way of 'interesting' work.*

Once done, click **submit updates** and it will return you to the main details screen.

Edition Number is only needed if this is the 2nd or subsequent edition of the book. If this is the 1st edition DO NOT put the number 1 in. It is assumed.

Now it will ask you to fill in the primary author. That is **you** and this is where any **penname** you use will go in. The section immediately underneath that asks for contributors and has a box defaulted to author. That can be confusing as it looks like you have to fill in your details again. You don't. This is in case you have a co-author, or an illustrator or an editor etc. So if it is only you, you can ignore the contributor bit.

The next entry asks for a description of your book. This is most often the 'back blurb' that would appear on the back cover of a paperback but in this case of course, as an eBook, you don't have a back cover so this is what will appear on the Amazon sales page. Take your time figuring this out. You need to distil the hook of your book into a paragraph or two and it can be a massively difficult task for an author to do. Seek out help from your writing friends if need be as this description is very, very important. It will be the only thing, apart from your cover, that you have to entice readers to buy your book. So take your time to get it right. You can format it using the toolbar on the description box. But do not go mad. Bold and italics work, do not pepper it with multiple fonts.

Next is a statement about rights. You wrote your book, therefore you own the rights so normally you would tick that option, but if you are publishing an amended work that is already in the public domain you would select that option. Need to know more about public domain works? Well, KDP offers a handy link to explain it more fully.

Then come **Keywords**. Now… there are whole volumes of other books, blog articles, online forums and discussion groups about the validity and impact of Amazon keywords and their direct link to you getting your book found in the right places by the right people. Amazon after all is just a massive search engine with products attached. Search engines work on keywords. Amazon is no different, therefore the selection of keywords is vital. According to KDP:

Search keywords help readers find your book when they browse the Amazon site. You can enter keywords or short phrases that describe your book and are relevant to its content. The best keywords are those that do not repeat words in the title, category, or description, as these are already used to help readers find your book. Some types of keywords are prohibited and may result in content being removed from sale.

Added to that explanation is a KDP link to a whole raft of advice and information on the selection of keywords which I don't intend to regurgitate here. Also, I am not a bona fide expert in the selection of keywords so the best advice I can give is try some out, monitor your sales and adjust them as you see fit, but a simple Google search will reveal more than you ever wanted to know about this subject, so happy browsing.

Once done you can then select the categories your book should be listed in. Again, fairly straightforward. If you have a sci-fi book that is set in an apocalyptic world the most likely categories for you might be:

- Fiction: Science Fiction: Apocalyptic & Post-Apocalyptic
- Fiction: Dystopian

Choose wisely as these will have an impact on the genre of books you are up against within the Amazon sales rankings.

At this point, if it is intended as a children's book you set the age group and then you set your release date.

IMPORTANT - If you plan to release as soon as you have

uploaded it then select 'I am ready to release my book now', but… I thoroughly recommend you choose to set a pre-order date. That way you will have time to begin a marketing campaign and a thoroughly well-thought out release strategy for your book. Seriously, it takes time to build momentum so don't try to rush headlong into getting your book out there. Set a realistic pre-order date (3-months away is good) and then begin to get the word out. The other thing with a future date is that all pre-orders will be accumulated and counted on the day of release. This should boost your standing in best-seller lists significantly. Without over-stressing it – if you can, **set a pre-order release**. One thing to note though. If you set a pre-order date make sure you have the final version of your book uploaded in plenty of time and **DO NOT** miss it. Amazon do not forgive easily if you withdraw from a pre-order. In fact they will bar you from having another one for a year. So don't mess this up. Set a pre-order that makes it easy for you to achieve. Do not be setting one while you are still writing your manuscript…

Save and continue onto the next page, **Kindle eBook content**. This is the place where you upload your interior and cover files. Before you do that you have the option of setting Digital Rights Management. This is meant to be an encryption method that prevents someone illegally copying and sharing your product across devices, but there are numerous and easy ways to crack it, so if someone wanted to rip your books off they could without too much effort. It also prevents someone who has bought your work from sharing it and that can be frustrating for them. So an inconvenience to some "good players" and if "bad players" really wanted to break it, they could. For those reasons I tend to leave it off. Be warned, whatever you choose – it cannot be changed in the future, so it's either on or off for ever.

Now you are ready to upload your interior file. This can be in a range of formats, but the easiest is a standard Microsoft®

Word document that KDP's internal conversion engine will turn into a Kindle specific formatted file. To make the conversion simple you do need to have a properly formatted Word document to begin with and as mentioned earlier, we will cover that in a later chapter. (Take the time to look at it, as it will save you a whole heap of hassle…)

If your book is graphics heavy and you wish to lock all the pages down so they are exactly as you see them on your screen then it is recommended you upload a KPF file. To make one of those you need to download Kindle's Textbook or Children's Book Creator programs, but that falls outside the main theme of this book so I won't be exploring it any further. However, KDP offers a help page on it and within Creator itself there is a simple to follow user guide.

And if it is REALLY complex formatting, (tables, graphs, footnotes, images all over the place etc) then you will probably need to employ a professional conversion service. Even my company doesn't do that level of conversion and we use a great outfit based in the UK, so again, if that's what you need, get in touch.

Once your interior file is uploaded (click on upload eBook manuscript and select your file) it will be put through the KDP conversion process. While you wait you can upload your cover.

Yes, KDP offer a cover creator that you could use to make your cover but my firm opinion is… **DON'T!!**

In fact, I shall reiterate it, DO NOT do that.

Most covers self-produced using these type of cover creator engines look amateurish at best and childish at worst. Please, please, *please* use a proper cover designer and make your cover as professional and appropriate to genre as you can. The old cliché of 'Don't judge a book by its cover' may well be a great way to live your life, but sadly, 99.9% of readers will absolutely judge a book by its cover. It has to tie in with its genre, or it has to be so amazing that it can break the genre rules and get away with it. The latter is unlikely so you will begin to understand why so many crime thrillers have dark silhouetted figures walking away in a cityscape or landscape. It's a shorthand way to shout out to readers that like that genre, "Hey, over here. I'm a book you'll like."

One final word about eBook covers. They are normally required to be in jpeg format, be in RGB colour mode, at least 300 dpi and usually best when 1600 pixels by 2400 pixels. If you do not understand how to make a graphics file like that, then get yourself a graphics designer who does. It's that simple.

As soon as the interior and cover are uploaded and once you have satisfied yourself that the spelling errors that may have been found are either acceptable and you click to ignore them, or they are not acceptable, so you fix them in your manuscript and re-upload, then go ahead and preview your file using the KDP previewer. It is quite cool and very practical. You can check out your table of contents (again covered in a later chapter) and you can verify the free-flow nature of your book. Once satisfied, exit out of the previewer back to the main screen, by clicking on **Book Details** up in the top left of the screen.

Oh, and once back on the 'Content' screen, this might be where you get to see spelling errors that had previously not been shown by KDP (sometimes it takes it a while to report them in a new manuscript). Again, ignore them or fix and re-upload.

The last thing to do on this page is to add your Kindle book details. If you have a publisher name, more properly called your Imprint, registered then you would enter it here and you can also enter an ISBN. At which point we shall have to discuss ISBNs.

ISBNs and ASINs

The International Standard Book Number is the strange number that appears with a barcode on the back of a paperback or hardback book. ISBNs are required for every different format of book. You need one ISBN for a paperback that is 7" x 4". A different one if you have a paperback that is 8" x 5.25" And a different one again if you have a hardback. And a different one again for the audio version.

You do not need to have a different ISBN if you simply reissue the same size of book with a different cover image.

Most PoD companies will allow you to use one of their ISBNs for free. Once more I would recommend that you… DON'T!! Their ISBNs will be restrictive and will limit where and when you can distribute your book. So what should you do? Simple. Buy your own.

Each country has a single source outlet for where you can buy them. In the UK it is Nielsen UK ISBN Agency, in the US and Australia it is Thorpe and Bowker. Find yours by a Google search. The cost of a single ISBN can be a bit off-putting, but if you buy ten the price usually drops through the floor. If you are going to be releasing through paperback, KDP and D2D you'll need a couple at least. Register with the agency for your country, buy the ISBNs and register yourself as the Publisher of Record. It adds a layer of professionalism to the Indie author. So do it.

However, don't buy the barcodes. They will be provided free

of charge by the likes of Ingram Spark and KDP and you can use them with no issues, they are not restrictive. They are simply generated for you, so do not buy barcodes.

Right – deep breath – it's gonna get complicated… E-Books need ISBNs too, but not a barcode. However, if you *only* want your eBook to be for sale on Amazon, then you don't need an ISBN as Amazon will assign an Amazon Standard Identification Number (ASIN). But, you can also assign your own ISBN to an Amazon version. Whilst ISBNs are not mandatory and do not provide copyright on a work, it does uniquely identify the work and is used internationally across the book trade and library sector. So if you want to be professional, use an ISBN.

Given all those rules, if I bring out a Kindle format and then I want to release through an aggregator to the likes of Apple and Kobo etc, the file that they receive will be an ePublication (ePub) format. (Don't stress, we shall cover all of these formats and how to make them later. For now, take it you will have two versions of your eBook).

Strictly, if I give the Kindle format an ISBN then the ePub should get a different one. In practise I don't. I assign a single ISBN as a generic 'eBook' format and I use that on the likes of Draft2Digital with the ePub format. I leave the ISBN on Amazon empty, but I put in my publisher name in the space allocated. That's it. All clear?

The bottom line is this; if you are only going to publish your book as an eBook through KDP you don't need an ISBN.

Now, let's fill in the last of the information needed and put your book into the world…

Kindle eBook Pricing

Select **Save and Continue** and we go to the last page of the KDP interface for uploading your eBook. This is where you set the price. You first get asked if you wish to enrol in KDP select.

KDP Select is Amazon's exclusive little eBook club and if you choose to enrol into it you will only be allowed to distribute your eBook to Amazon, so remember that. The enrolment period is set at three months, meaning you will be locked in for at least 90 days. Then you can exit out or stay in. And what does KDP Select do for you? Well, as I said in Chapter 3 - Readers who are members of the Kindle Unlimited Program can download and read your book for 'free'. Of course they have paid a monthly membership so it isn't really free. You as the author get a percentage payout of the Kindle Unlimited fund for that month based on how many downloads and, crucially, how many actual pages of your book were read. For those top selling or top 'borrowed' authors there are bonus payments given at the end of each month. Basically, people can borrow your book for a subscription and you get paid if they read it. You can also benefit from sales promotions and a few other "bonus features" that Amazon add to from time to time. There is a very comprehensive section all about it, if you click on the Learn More button provided on the screen.

I have some books enrolled in it and most are not. You need to investigate the benefits and make your own choice. If you only have one book, I would recommend not being in it and to "go wide" by using the likes of Draft2Digital and therefore not restrict yourself to just Amazon. Okay – onwards…

You are next asked which territories you want to sell in and for the vast majority of Indies that will be worldwide. If you are not sure, check out the links that KDP has available.

Then it is time to set your sales price. As mentioned earlier,

KDP offers 70% royalties for authors on eBooks. It also offers 35% royalties and you may wonder why you would choose the lower amount. Surely that is nonsensical. Well, you can only get 70% if your book is priced between $2.99 and $9.99 US. That isn't going to be much of an issue as most Indies will be pitching their books at the $3.99 or $4.99 mark and therefore are able to enjoy 70% rates.

The only other reason you might drop to 35% is that all Kindle books get charged a 'delivery' cost for the amount of bandwidth used to send the book out to the buyer's Kindle or Kindle App. If your book is very graphics heavy this delivery charge could be quite substantial. Were that to be the case, the 35% rate does not charge for delivery and so it may be that you end up with more resultant royalties than if you were on 70%.

To help you decide, all the separate market place prices can be set individually or tied to the US price. To do that, click where it says 'Other marketplaces' and play around with your pricing and your royalty rate until you are satisfied. Then save the prices and move on. One final thing about pricing. Once set, you can change it at any time, even after publication, but BEWARE!!

Don't fool about with pricing if you are in a pre-order phase. Set it and leave it until your publication date passes. If you were to reduce the price during a pre-order, all orders, even those made at the higher price point, will get it at the lowest price during the period.

Book lending is locked if you choose the 70% royalty rate so that is not an option for most. Then there is a terms and conditions statement and finally, the yellow button at the bottom that says… 'Publish Your Kindle eBook'. If you are ready, click it. Your pre-order (or final book) will show up on Amazon within 48-72 hours, most times much quicker. Then all you need to do is get your marketing in place to generate all the interest that you can. Hope for the whirlwind of readers' enthusiasm to sweep you up, receive multiple movie offers for your book's adaptation and retire to your own Caribbean island… Of course you will have to track all those sales, and to do that, you need reports.

Kindle Reports

The KDP reporting interface underwent a major change in 2022, but thankfully, whoever oversees Amazon KDP software development knows what they are doing. It is still easy to use, intuitive, straightforward and simply, **THE BEST** indy book reporting tool out there. It now covers print and eBooks, so this is your one-stop-shop for KDP sales.

As soon as your book is released, you can access all the sales figures through the **Report**s option on your KDP menu.

Initially the screen opens on a dashboard, from which you can see today's snapshot. Clicking on **View Orders** (or on **Orders** in the menu to the left) takes you to a fully customisable order view, where you can select by format, author, title, country of sale etc etc etc.

There is also a screen for pre-orders and a royalty estimator and a plethora of other views to tell you all you ever wanted to know about sales of your book.

The reports are detailed, customisable and self-explanatory. All in all, they are incredibly intuitive, so have a look at the various options available.

And with that, we're done with KDP eBooks, although we will come back later to discuss KDP paperbacks. For now though, it's time to look at an aggregator service for eBooks.

5

Draft2Digital Aggregator Service

To reiterate, an aggregator service is simply an interface that allows you to upload your book and cover to a single place, prior to it being distributed to a number of online retailers. My preferred choice is Draft2Digital (D2D) and this chapter will take you through how to use their services.

Before we get into the nuts and bolts of the D2D system, I need to point out that they offer a lot of conversion services for your book. In fact, if you want them to, they will convert your book for you, add in-design options, front matter (those bits that come before the start of your first chapter, such as title and copyright), automated end matter (those things like a list of the other books you have written, your author bio and useful marketing tools such as book teasers). Their interior file options are very comprehensive and they only need a word document as a source.

With that said, I tend not to use their conversion services, not because they aren't good, but because I developed my own way of converting my books, it works, is error free and therefore I go with the adage, *'If it ain't broke, don't fix it.'*

To follow my way, all you need is a shareware (as in free) software program called Calibre. However, we'll come to that in a later chapter. For now, let's take a look at the D2D interface. To begin, either do a Google search for Draft2Digital or go to www.draft2digital.com - ah! this is where I should put a different link... I usually forget... But... if you go to:

https://www.draft2digital.com/tbre

and sign up that way, then I would get a referral fee for the first year of your membership. It's free to you and paid direct by D2D, so, if you want to keep me in the coffee and donuts lifestyle I have become accustomed to, then sign up through my link. Or not. Your choice. My diet could probably benefit from less donuts...

Either way, once there, start by registering your account (the big red sign up button at the top right). This takes you to a first screen that is your details. All straightforward enough and once you agree to their terms of service you will be prompted to login to your new account.

The D2D interface is refreshingly uncluttered. It has a top menu of support options, Frequently Asked Questions, Blog links, Books2Read, Partner links and a Contact Us option. Under these is a link to your account section, their reporting options and a highlighted button that says, My Books. This, obviously enough, is where you click to begin to add your books, but before that you want to go to your account section.

In here are quite a few options, some you probably won't bother setting and a few that you really should (including author bio, that we will mention later), but the most important details to complete are of course under Payment Options. Click in here and setup your bank account or your other preferred method of payment.

D2D can use Paypal and/or Payoneer as an alternative to a bank account. Some of the payment methods have threshold amounts in US dollars, $100 for cheques, $20 for Payoneer, $10 for international direct deposit, and $0 for Paypal or US direct deposit. One word of caution, if setting up an Australian bank for payment, ensure you monitor the first transaction into your account. If there is an issue with it coming through, contact D2D support and they will route it a different way. It isn't a huge issue and I am sure they are probably well on top of it now, but worth bearing in mind. When mine went AWOL, D2D had it sorted inside a week and there have been no more problems.

You will also see on the payment page a Tax Interview button. Funnily enough, the very same type of interview you completed for KDP. I'm not going to repeat what we have covered before. Suffice to say, take your time, answer all the questions and enter the same Tax ID you used for KDP.

Returning to your account page, you will see a link for Universal Book Links. These are a neat idea arranged by Books2Read that will allow you to use a single web address, or Universal Resource Locator (URL) for your titles. That way any potential readers you want to advertise to are taken to a single page which has all the online links for your eBooks. You can even customise the links and add your own 'ending' to the URL. For example, www.books2read.com/FaceValue takes you to the page for my novel Face Value. There you will find links to all the places online you can buy the eBook, including the Amazon link, even though I don't use D2D to distribute my book to Amazon (because I use KDP). And, if when you go there it only has the Amazon link, it will be because I have enrolled in KDP select for a few months (yeah, I know, I can swap in and out).

The single URL is a good idea, as are the other innovations that D2D have added over the last few months, including book tabs and author pages. All of these you can customise as you see fit, but of course you can only do that once you have uploaded your first book, so let's look at how you do that.

Edit Book – Details

Click on the red button, **My Books** and on the next screen, click on the red button, **Add New Book**.

If you have your cover art, check the box and upload it. If you don't have it yet you will not be able to schedule a book release within 10 days. I recommend getting your cover art first. Again, it is an eBook, so it is the front cover only, in the format they ask for: 1600x2400 or larger, JPG or PNG.

Once loaded, enter in the title, author name, publisher name, (you may have to add a new author or new publisher if you haven't taken the time to add them in the account section of the site – it's okay, just add them now as you go through the form). D2D provide handy help popup notes, so the process is fairly straightforward.

If this is a series the book number in the series goes into the Volume Number entry.

All in all, most of the same stuff as you have already filled in on KDP will work here, but there is a difference regarding the categories, or as they are called on D2D - BISAC Subjects.

For a start they are different to the categories available on Amazon and you can choose up to five against the two you could choose in KDP. Where there is a plus sign next to the topic you can click on it and drill down to the subject you think best describes your book. The search "Filter BISACS" is a good tool and works well.

The other main difference is that you can choose a lot more than seven keywords in the box labelled 'Search Terms' but again, think long and hard about what will best bring likely readers to your book.

Once done, click on **START EBOOK**.

At the top of the page is the place where you upload your interior manuscript. As I mentioned, that can be a word document if you want D2D to do the conversion for you, but it can also be an ePub formatted file that is already in a finished state to be distributed. I'll explain how to make one of these in Chapter 10, but regardless of your file type, all you do is select browse, navigate to where the file is on your PC and upload it. While you wait for the processing to complete, enter in your chosen release date (if you have a cover then this can be anytime, but make it the same release date as you used on KDP). Then enter in your description (same as KDP). If there are additional collaborators that you are splitting payments to, add them and if the book is an omnibus edition of a bundle of books, check the box.

Add in your eBook ISBN (as discussed earlier, you need an ISBN for this format) and then, once your file is processed, click on save and continue.

Edit Book – Layout

On this page are the check boxes that allow you to include the automated material that D2D can do on your behalf. These are things like author bio (that you would have to set up initially within the account page) and they'll even include a copyright page for you. One thing you might want to tick, if you know you have more books coming out, is the 'New Release Email Notifications Signup' that is another way to build a following of readers. Admittedly not the best way, as D2D get the email addresses instead of you, but every little helps. If and when you bring out a new book, D2D will email anyone who has signed up for notifications about you. To do that the D2D interface will add an additional page at the end of your book prompting readers to sign up.

Next to that is a sample of the chapters that they have detected within your file. These will be set exactly as you wanted them if you uploaded an ePub or they will be set as the D2D converter detected them if you uploaded a raw Word file. Mostly, if you have set up your source document correctly (as we'll cover in Chapter 9) these should have come through in a fit state, but depending on how D2D has interpreted your file you may find some issues. Don't despair. If the chapters showing are not what you expected, click on the appropriately labelled button, 'Help! These aren't my Chapters!' Once in there you will be given a range of options to attempt to pick the correct layout. If it still doesn't resolve to the correct chapter headings you can submit a request to the D2D layout team. Thing is, if you properly format it in the first place and/or convert it using Calibre, then you won't have to worry about this issue. As soon as you have the chapters the way you want them, click on save and continue.

Edit Book – Preview

If you uploaded a raw Word file then the system will offer you an on-screen preview with a whole host of layout options on the right hand side of the screen. These allow you to modify the style of the 'section breaks'. These are the gaps between 'scenes' in a standard novel. They can be an extra space or the common three asterisks *** or much more fancy styles. The D2D style options offered for converted books will change these in line with genre themes.

If you don't have section breaks you may wonder what the different styles are doing, but they are consistently correct. You can also choose to add drop capitals to your layout. My advice is if you have used D2D to convert your book, take your time to click onto each option and see what it does to your manuscript.

Once satisfied, or if you uploaded an ePub file directly, D2D will ask you to download and check the Mobi and ePub files they have now generated for their internal systems. **Do it**. Make sure that the files you are about to approve meet your requirements. If you do not have an in built Mobi or ePub viewer there are even links to download one of those too. Having reviewed the files and approved them, check the box that says the same, save and continue, and move on to the price setup for your book. And a final reminder, MOBI format will be disappearing sooner rather than later, so if you don't see a reference to it, don't panic.

Edit Book – Publish

The last stage in the D2D interface is where you set the price and the channels of distribution for your eBook.

As you can see on the screen, D2D allows you to choose which channels you distribute to by a simple check box mechanism. Obviously, if you have set your own book up in KDP you do NOT check the Amazon box.

The screen is split into three sections. The top is for sales channels. The next is for subscription services (where people pay a monthly or annual subscription and can download quantities of books) and the bottom section is for Overdrive and other suppliers of eBooks to libraries. A quick note on libraries. D2D recommend you set your library price to two times your retail price. I have to admit, I'm not completely sure the reason behind that, but I think it is because libraries receive a bigger percentage discount. I don't check the Hoopla option as you cannot change your retail price with them in the future and I don't like that idea.

That brings us to pricing. At the very top of this screen there is a space for you to enter the price of your book in US dollars. There is also a button that says 'Manage Territorial Prices'. If you click on that it will allow you to set individual prices for other countries. Now, why would you do that? Well, rather the same as with the KDP price setup. If you set your book to be 3.99 in US, that can generate a less than round number in other currencies. You might want it to be 3.99 pounds and 3.99 euro, so this individual setting of prices allows you to do that. In D2D all you have to do is check the box next to the country you want to set and enter the figures. Once happy, click Change Pricing.

Set your library price and then click submit. Your book will either go live, or if set for a future release date it will go on pre-order at the various outlets that support pre-orders.

At that point you will have released an eBook into the world on a wide array of distribution channels. Well done!

However, now and in the future you will want to know how many you have sold and how much $$$$ you can expect!

D2D Reporting

Under the menu, **Reports**, D2D supply a range of information, from the number of readers signed up to follow your new releases through to the things you probably want to know most about, how many books have you sold and how much money are you due.

The great thing is that both of those are listed bright and clear on the opening page of the reports section, but remember, your royalties paid to D2D may not become payable to you for a month or more depending on how fast the sales channels pay out. According to the official D2D policy:

Our digital stores all have different policies on their payments. Most of them delay payments by about 60 days after the end of the month in which the sale happens. We can't control that, but whatever we get (no matter when the sale happened), we'll send along to you in your next monthly payment.

So be patient. You'll get it, just not as fast as you might want.

Also on the left hand side are a range of reporting options that are all fully customisable and most of which will display on screen. I especially like the Raw Sales Data report that shows where each title was sold and through which channel. If you click on show details, or choose to download the csv file (small link to the top right of the screen) you will also see the country of origin of the purchase. It really is a most comprehensive report.

The account ledger is also very handy when it comes to tax time as it shows payments due and tax withheld.

§

(Yep, I'm a fancy section break – more about me later…)

You now have your eBook out and about in the world, or at least set up as a pre-order. So what about your book-book? For eBooks are great, but there is nothing like holding a physical copy of your own book in your hand. To do that, read on…

6

Trim Size

First things first, before we look at how you are going to publish a physical book, you need to decide on the size you want your book to be. This is called the 'Trim Size' and is your starting point. Now granted, you probably thought, "Well, I'd like my book to be book size please…" But the amount of diversity within that one decision is mind boggling. It also gets a little complicated by the fact that certain sizes won't be allowed by certain PoD providers. Sooooo…

The easiest way to figure out what trim size you want your book to be, is to go and look at some books. Be that on your own bookshelf or in a library or a bookshop. Find one that you think is the right size for you, get a ruler and measure it. Yeah, I know, hardly rocket science is it…

If it is a hardback, be careful, as it is the inside size of the page we are after, not the outside overlap of the cover. That's that then. You have your size, in either inches or millimetres. It might be 8.268" x 11.693" (210mm x 297mm) or what we know as A4. It might be 4" x 6" (102mm x 152mm) or it could be all manner of things in between.

In the publishing industry there are some formats that are taken as the "standards". One of these, in fact the most common for paperbacks, is the A-Format, otherwise known as 'mass market' paperback. It is the small size book you see in most bookshops, especially at airports and measures 4.37" x 7.0" (110mm x 178mm). If you go get one of these from a shelf and take a look inside you will usually see that the paper within is a cream colour, a kind of off-white called 'crème'. It could be described as all sorts of shades, but it certainly isn't 'true white'.

I'm delighted to report that, after many years of not supporting that size, KDP and Ingram Spark now allow it as a selectable option. (Albeit in KDP you have to enter it as a custom size). KDP will publish it on crème paper. Ingram will use groundwood, (thin Eggshell colour) the traditional paper of mass paperbacks.

If that small size is not for you, then all the other standard trade sizes are there, like 5" x 8" and 5.25" x 8" (my particular choice for paperback) all the way up to the format known as 'Royal' 6.14" x 9.21" (234 x 156mm) which is the 'big' hardback layout you would see for most 'new releases' in bookshops.

Before we go on, a small note about this issue of crème versus white paper. It certainly isn't a firm and fixed rule, but it tends to be that text books and kids illustrated books will be produced on white paper, with novels and some hardbacks, regardless of subject, being printed on crème. What's the best rule of thumb for you? It's the same as the trim size; find a book similar to your own and take a look inside. Then replicate it as close as you can.

With your trim size settled on you then have to figure out margins. Once more, you can spend quite a lot of time doing this or you can elect to use a very handy shortcut. As you will see later, if you choose a standard size within KDP, they have downloadable, pre-formatted templates that are already set up for the correct margin sizes. If you are not using a size set within KDP, then Google is once more going to be your friend. Just make sure that for paperback or hardback you use mirror margins.

This allows the 'inside' margin on each opposing page to be set properly. It has the strange effect of making it look like your text is 'jumping' from the left to the right on alternate pages, but it will end up with both pages being balanced within the physical book.

To reiterate, if you want your book to be black and white type with no internal illustrations, printed on crème paper with a matt finish to the cover (we will expand on matt versus gloss later), then first of all, go to KDP and Ingram and check that they support those options in the size you want. For me, I had it easy. My crime novels are black and white text on crème paper with a matt cover in an overall book size of 8.00 inches by 5.25 inches. The resultant line within Ingram looks like this:

B&W 5.25 x 8 in or 203 x 133mm Perfect Bound on Crème w/Matte Lam.

As in, a perfect bound paperback on crème paper with a matte laminate finish to the cover.

To make that happen, I went to KDP, (Google KDP Templates) downloaded one of their Word templates for a book that was 8"×5.25" and this template document became my starting point. Downloading a template is by far the easiest way to manage your interior file. The same is true for your cover.

Cover Template

I mentioned in the preceding paragraphs that you can choose to have a glossy finish or a matt finish to your cover. Once more, your best guide will be to look at similar books within the genre you will be publishing in and see which is most prevalent, or which you prefer. Then replicate it. Bear in mind that Sci-Fi tend to be glossy. Children's illustrated books are definitely glossy. Crime thrillers, usually matte. After that decision, you will need a cover template.

As KDP provides you with an interior template, so they and

IngramSpark's parent company, Lightning Source, will provide you with cover templates. For reasons best known to themselves though, for a given identical trim size, Amazon and Ingram's cover templates are fractionally different, so you will have to download both. (You could argue and rant at this – or shrug your shoulders and say, "Ah well…").

The two cover template generators allow your graphics designer to make a perfectly fitting cover in 'indesign' or PDF. You will need to ask them to export it back to you in PDF. That makes it the easiest for upload later. The only snag is that to set the cover up properly you will need to know exactly how many pages are in your book, so that the spine width can be set properly. That means whilst your designer can mock up some draft covers for you, they will need to wait until you have completed your book to make the final version.

To use the Lightning Source cover generator, visit here:
https://myaccount.lightningsource.com/Portal/Tools/ CoverTemplateGenerator

As you will see, that template generator automatically adds a barcode matched to your ISBN. Your cover designer will be able to take that barcode and copy it for use on your Amazon cover. Perfect!

To download the Amazon cover, go here:
https://kdp.amazon.com/en_US/cover-templates

7

Amazon's KDP for Paperback

To begin, a little recap.

Amazon's KDP has global reach, their interface allows you to practise with your interior setup as much as you like, they don't have any setup fees, they do have relatively good print quality and they will supply your book directly to the biggest bookshop on the planet, Amazon.

Just don't let them try to distribute it to any others. As I've already mentioned, book shops won't want to order your book from a major (***the*** major) competitor. As you'll see later on, within KDP is a distribution section. I would really recommend that you only choose Amazon store distribution. Turn the expanded distribution off. That way you will get the best of both worlds. Amazon distribute to Amazon with excellent royalty rates and IngramSpark, who we will look at in the next chapter, will look after your wider distribution.

I use both with success and have definitely benefited from Ingram's Melbourne printing operations that allow me to order books for personal appearances and book launches within Australia at a much reduced cost. That said, I started exclusively with KDP because their interface was so easy to navigate.

If you already have a Kindle version of your book setup as

per the instructions given earlier, then you can fast track a lot of the details by clicking **+Create paperback**. This will copy over all the details from the Kindle to the paperback and save you a whole heap of time. However, I shall assume you haven't done that, so you can see all the things you need to put in. If you fast-track, then you can still follow these steps, but without all the typing.

Right then! Let's begin. If you haven't already, setup your Amazon KDP **account** as per the instructions in Chapter 4.

Once complete and all is saved, return to your member dashboard by clicking on the Bookshelf link at the top of the screen and either click on **+Create**, then chose to create a paperback, or as I said, if you already have a Kindle version, click on **+Create paperback** next to it.

Start Your New Project

Either way you will be taken to the first of three screens, Paperback Details.

The paperback interface is intuitive and follows almost exactly the eBook layout, (so for the details about series adding etc, refer to Chapter 4) but for now, a quick recap on contributors.

Halfway down the page it will ask you to fill in the primary author. That is you and this is where any penname you use will go in. The section immediately underneath that asks for contributors and has a box defaulted to author. That can be confusing as it looks like you have to fill in your details again. You don't. This is in case you have a co-author, or an illustrator or an editor etc. So if it is only you, ignore this bit.

The description, publishing rights, keywords and categories is exactly as per the eBook interface, so refer back to Chapter 4 for any queries on those.

At this point, it will ask you if your book contains Adult Content – this is a reference to mainly adult erotica, so if your book is full of content unsuitable for those under 18, select yes. My crime novels, although containing death and swearing get a NO at this point as they don't contain *that* type of adult content.

Select **save and continue** to move on and you will be taken to the Paperback Content page.

We have already discussed ISBNs. Suffice to say, KDP will offer you one of theirs, **don't use it**, buy and use one of your own. Add in the Imprint name you used when you bought your ISBNs. This may have been a company name or your name – but **IMPORTANT** - make sure they match, otherwise KDP will not let you move on to the next screen later on.

Then there is a bit of a strange thing. It lists a publication date but you can't set one in the future. Instead, leave it blank and move on but beware for later. Currently (Sep 2022) you cannot set a pre-release date for KDP paperbacks. It is quite annoying and perhaps they will change it, but for now, we'll go through the rest of the setup and talk more about release dates later.

Next are the selection of print options. Standard fiction novels will tend to be black and white interior with crème paper, but you can choose your own preferences. Then choose your trim size from the **Select a different size** box if you need to. Page bleed for standard fiction is a NO, but would be a yes for illustrated books where you want the illustration to go right to the sides of the pages. Then you can pick gloss or matt cover finish as per your preference.

Manuscript

The on-screen instructions now prompt you to upload a document in a variety of available formats. You can upload your completed manuscript in its native Word format, but be aware that occasionally the page breaks get altered a little in the conversion process. It isn't a massive issue as you can go through and resolve any discrepancies, but it is easier to upload a **PDF** version of your Word document. That way it will be set exactly as you want it to be. How you produce a PDF version is covered off in the 'Formatting your Word Document' chapter later on.

Once the upload of your interior file is complete we can move on to the cover.

Book Cover

You have the option of using the Cover Creator or uploading a cover you already have, in a print-ready PDF format only.

DO THE LATTER - ALWAYS DO THE LATTER

The cover creator is a convenience but looks like amateur hour, so get a proper designer to design your cover and upload it as a PDF, properly sized within the KDP template that you will have downloaded earlier.

Select the check box if it already has a barcode added by your designer or select to add one if not. I stress again, have your designer place the barcode. Amazon's automatic placement gives you little control over where it ends up on the rear cover.

Then upload the file.

Bear in mind one of the main reasons for doing your own cover is you will have complete design control over the spine of the book and that is important.

You see spines are a strange concept. You don't really take much notice of them once you have bought a book, but in the shop it may be the only thing you see. Therefore, it needs to 'pop' off the shelf. It also needs to have a space at the bottom of it. Usually this is where the publisher's logo would be placed. It forces the title of the book and the author's name up the spine. Why on earth is that important? Well, in a library they will stick a catalogue sticker over the foot of the spine normally covering that space or logo, but if your author name or title is extending all the way down to the bottom, that sticker will cover them instead. Who would think of such things? I know I certainly didn't and that was exactly the problem my first book suffered from. My name was covered up by a sticker. As I said, most of us Indies learnt through trial and error. That was a definite error. Don't do the same.

Additionally, this print book cover has a back. That means you need a back blurb. You know, the thing that you read in a bookshop before you make a purchase. It is a distillation of your book and a hook for the reader. It is also very hard to write if you have slaved for months or years on a book and are now asked to sum it all up in a short paragraph or two. You may need to seek outside help. Whatever way you manage it, make sure it goes on your back cover and if you were lucky enough later to get reviews by major industry players, then you can add them on here too.

When your front, back and spine are done, upload it and once more for effect… *Please get a proper cover designer and upload a print-ready PDF.* Once you have, the KDP system will begin to process it and you need to press the Launch Previewer button. Once you click on it, wait, for a few minutes, sometimes more, whilst KDP formats and renders your paperback in a brilliant preview system that lets you "see" how your paperback will be laid out.

A small dialogue box will pop up telling you it is 'working' followed by more messages to inform you of the stages being assessed.

Once the automated print checks are completed, the interior reviewer opens to a virtual rendering of your book. Any issues are listed down the left hand side and you have a couple of viewing options along the bottom. These set the page to two page view (the most realistic book layout) and thumbnail view (handy for making sure all your page breaks and chapters are flowing the way you intended). You can also, by clicking on a page, zoom in to see any fine details and move around by "grabbing" the page with your mouse. All in all this is a superb piece of software and the beauty is it will allow you to see a vast array of issues before you spend any money printing a proof copy of your book.

Take your time. Go through it carefully. Normally you should go through it at least two or three times. Note down any changes you need to make, then select the option in the bottom right of the screen to go back and make changes (Exit Print Previewer). Revise your original file on your computer, upload a new version of your interior file and do the review process again.

You can repeat this as often as you need to until you either have no issues reported or, occasionally, where you are prepared to ignore the issues and save anyway. This is unusual but it might be if you had a poorer quality illustration that was being reported as not meeting the recommended DPI settings, but it is the only copy you have and you want it in your book. You can force it to be ignored.

Either way, eventually you will have an interior file that you are content with. Once that is the case you can select **Approve**, at which point the resultant screen will show you the print costs for your book in US Dollars at the bottom right of the screen.

To move on, select **save and continue**. You will not be able to move on until the interior and cover review of your manuscript has been completed in an error-free state and you have approved the manuscript and cover.

I thoroughly recommend you use the KDP paperback interior review process as much as you can. It is free no matter how many revisions you upload. It is quick and it is as good a software rendition of your physical book as you are likely to get.

Once you approve it and select save and continue we can set the pricing and distribution channels.

Territories

First you are asked to set the territories you hold the distribution rights for. You can select individual countries, or more usually, as this is your book and you own all the rights, you will simply select All Territories (Worldwide). There are clickable links to explain these rights next to the alternative selections if you are unsure.

Distribution and Pricing

There are currently twelve market places for individual price setting on Amazon KDP and you can choose which one is primary. Choose the one you are most comfortable in dealing with as a currency. It is only there as a guide for you. Once selected you can set the sales price for your book. As in you set that price and all the rest of the international prices are set to follow it. Or, you can set all prices individually. Whichever way you choose you will also see the royalty breakdown you will get dependent on the price you set. Paperbacks sold through KDP earn 60% royalty rates after the cost of printing and distributing your book are deducted from the Recommended Retail Price you choose. Play around with the numbers, see what you can get, but also bear in mind your book size and likely price points for a book of similar size and genre. Yes, you could set your 100-page short novella to sell at 100 dollars, but who is likely to buy it?

You will also see the option for allowing Amazon to provide your book to their expanded distribution. Don't select this. We will provide expanded distribution through Ingram and so we will not use this option within Amazon. By the way, if you have setup your Ingram version first, then Amazon KDP will "recognise" the ISBN in use and display this message:

The information that was entered makes your book ineligible for Expanded Distribution. To be eligible, your book must have an ISBN that hasn't been submitted for distribution to another service.

There are also trim size requirements that depend on paper type that might prevent KDP offering the expanded distribution option.

One last thing about the pricing, the good news is that you can change the prices in here at any time and the change will filter through to Amazon stores fairly rapidly. This is a big advantage over other PoD suppliers.

Complete Setup

You now have the option to request a proof copy of your book from Amazon and **I THOROUGHLY RECOMMEND** you do this.

Click on request a proof copy and Amazon will generate a copy that you can order through your normal Amazon customer account. You select the Marketplace of your order (US, Canada, UK, Australia or a number of European countries) and how many proof copies you want. Then you submit proof request. Once done, login to your Amazon customer account and go to your shopping cart. Your proof copy will await you. I'm pleased to report that the problem Amazon Australia had regarding this ordering option for Australian based authors seems to have been solved. All Amazon proofs will come out with an over-stamp of ***Proof Copy*** across the cover.

Publishing on KDP

You'll remember back a little while ago, I said that KDP wouldn't allow you to set a publishing date in the future. Therefore, if you want to publish your book on a certain day, perhaps to tie in with a Kindle pre-order date or an Ingram pre-order date (that we will look at later) you need to press 'Publish' in KDP on the actual day itself.

That seems straightforward enough, but be aware that the time KDP uses is Los Angeles time, or more correctly, US Pacific Time. So if you live in Australia or the UK or wherever else that isn't on Pacific Time and you want your book to be recorded as being published on a specific day, you need to wait until Pacific Time has caught up. As an example, if you were in Western Australia and you want your book published on let's say the 14th, you need to wait until 4pm on the 14th before hitting publish. That way it has gone past midnight Pacific Time. However, Amazon can take up to 72-hours to approve your paperback for release, so if you wait until the day, it might be a couple of days later when it is "published". It's a lottery. Take your chances. Personally I press publish 48-hours beforehand and usually it publishes on the day I want it to. Sometimes it is early. Sometimes, late.

If you are not ready to publish yet, then simply save as draft and wait patiently for your big day. When it comes around, click on the continue setup button next to your paperback version on your bookshelf and finally, when you are good and ready, click on publish your paperback.

Ordering Author Copies

Now your book is in the world, you can order your own copies. Why would you? Well, you may want some for family and friends, or you may need to take some to an author event like a book launch or a talk. Whatever the reason, on the Member Dashboard of KDP, to the right hand side of the title of your book is a link for ordering copies. In fact it is a button that says **Order author copies**.

Clicking on it takes you to the order screen. Here you can fill in the quantity of books you want (up to 999), the marketplace you want them to come from, US, UK, Italy etc. It will display the approximate cost and link to your Amazon customer account where the order will be placed, finalised and paid for.

Royalty Reports

Once your book is live the reporting of sales and royalties is displayed on the same interface as KDP eBooks as mentioned in Chapter 4.

Each report can be customised with regard to the date ranges being shown and each subsequent display can also be downloaded as an Excel spreadsheet.

The payment history report is especially handy as it shows the amount of tax withheld from payments made and the dates on which those payments were processed through to your individual payment method.

Revisions

The main strength of KDP is that for all PoD paperbacks and eBooks, the initial publication is completely free of charge. As are any revisions.

This means that should you discover an error in your manuscript or cover, or should you wish to add an additional page at the back of your book detailing other books you write later, you can simply go through the uploading, reviewing, proofing and publishing method as we have described. There are no fees and as soon as you proof and accept the book, the new version will be available on Amazon. Small amendments like these can usually be approved through the digital, online proofing tools without the need for a printed proof.

So that is your paperback online and for sale through Amazon. But what about selling to booksellers, be that other online distributors or bricks-and-mortar bookshops and what about hardbacks?[6] Well, that's where IngramSpark come in.

---

[6] Currently, September 2022, Amazon have a beta system for hardbacks. No doubt this will be fully up and running by 2023, if not sooner. But their trim sizes seem to be limited. Best to keep an eye on it.

8

IngramSpark

You're hopefully getting the hang of this now, so you will probably have already Googled IngramSpark or gone to www.ingramspark.com. Up in the top right is a link to **Create Account**.

But before you click on it, take a second or two to look at the screen you are on. There are four main menu links on the top bar which are well worth having a browse through. I especially recommend you take a good look at the 'Plan Your Book' section where you will see guides to genres, layouts, page sizes and trim sizes. It is all worthwhile information and the more you read and know, the more you will become a professional Indie.

A lot of this information you will now be familiar with. You can nod along as you already understand about trim sizes and colour of interior papers. Some of it will be new, but that's okay. In fact go and get a cup of tea, coffee or whatever your preferred beverage is and take a bit of time to browse around the Ingram site. There really is a wealth of interesting and pertinent information on there.

Once you are ready, it is time to open an account, so click on that **Create Account** link.

It is the same type of thing as you would expect, name address etc. Verify you aren't a robot. Get an activation email and click on it. The Ingram system will then prompt you that there are some global agreements you need to be aware of.

Global POD - Print-on-Demand (POD) services via our Lightning Source companies in the US, UK, AU, as well as the Global Connect and Espresso POD networks.

Global EBook - EBook distribution services to all of our EBook Distribution Partners except Amazon Kindle and Apple.

Amazon (Kindle) EBook (optional) - If you want to distribute your EBooks to Amazon Kindle. (You can opt out if you are uploading direct to Kindle).

Apple (Agency) EBook (optional) - If you want to distribute your EBooks to Apple's US and International iBooks and iTunes stores.

Just to clarify then. Ingram have a global Print on Demand distribution agreement that you must agree to. It doesn't actually mean you have to use them to distribute your books, but if you decide to later, then all is set fair.

Ingram also offer eBook conversion and distribution services. Once more, this doesn't mean you have to use them and in our case we won't be, as we will be using KDP and D2D, but you agree to it just in case you might change your mind later and it is a requirement to establish an Ingram account. So you have to.

They also have two separate and optional distribution agreements, one for distributing to Amazon Kindle (which is optional and as you are using KDP you won't need it) and one that allows them to distribute eBooks to Apple iBooks, (also optional and also not required as you are using Draft2Digital).

Up in the top right is a login link and that's where you click next. Once logged in you are prompted to accept the policy agreements, before being required to fill in additional information that identifies you.

Your Business name or Legal name is you. Contact name is probably also you. Form of business, well in most cases it will be a sole proprietor for Indies, but if you have setup a company or partnership to print under their banner then fill it in appropriately. The **'What Best Describes You'** is not a dating profile, but merely a way for them to ascertain your level of experience and what you are primarily here for. As a new Indie you will most likely answer, 'I've never published but am ready to publish now'.

Then there are a series of standard security questions, followed by the agreements we mentioned previously. Accept the top two for sure and the bottom two if you want.

The system then gives you the choice to go and visit your dashboard or finish setting up your account. I recommend finishing the setup. Otherwise you will have to go and do it later. So click on the yellow button, 'Finish Setting Up My Account'.

The first step is to choose the currency to be paid in. Standard enough choices but you must choose US dollars if you wish to use Paypal. I'm going to assume you choose the currency of the country you live in and then you click on add compensation information, which is a very posh way of saying, enter your bank details. Once that is done you can click to continue down in the bottom right. (A little point, if the round radio button won't select next to your country of choice, go ahead and add your banking details under that country and once you save them the radio button will become selected).

The next section is where you add a credit card so that Ingram can take payments against your account as and when required. This would be for book orders and for setup fees (which we will cover a bit later). For now, add a new card to allow you to move on. You can add alternate cards later. To shortcut the card screen when you are entering your details you can click on the 'Use My Default Address'. Be prepared to wait a while for the screen to refresh as it verifies you and your card details.

At that point you can then select to continue and this drops you into the Tax Information screens. Sadly, this is not as straightforward as KDP or D2D.

Depending on your country of residence you may have to add additional information. For example, in Australia, to fully use Ingram you need an ABN. If you haven't got one you can of course register for one from the Australian Government's Australian Business Register and if you do that yourself online there is no fee.

Once you have satisfied any additional information you can then go on to claim your US Tax Exemptions. BEWARE!! This is going to take you a while. You don't have to do this at the moment if you don't want to and it would only become important if you started selling a lot of books in the US, but there is no harm in doing it. You need to be prepared for something a lot different to the other tax interviews you have done so far. Thing is, if you start, you need to finish.

Click on the Claim US Tax Exemptions, then select Yes, then click continue.

Select the option that best fits you. If you are not living in the US and you are an Indie author then it is most likely to be the second option in the list, 'Claiming exemption based on resale and Business/Organization resides outside of the United States'. However, you have to choose the one that fits you. Once you have, click on continue.

You then go through a series of screens where you read and agree to Tax information as laid out by IngramSpark. You fill in your principal country of residence, and all other information before being presented with a list of tax forms.

As the screen says:

Based on the information you provided on the previous screen, you will need to review and sign the reseller form(s) listed below.

Click on the link(s) to download and print the form(s). As stated previously, several states require drop ship sales tax forms regardless of whether or not you are registered there. These states include IL, NY, PA and VA and their forms are also being provided to you.

You download the forms and follow the onscreen instructions. I shall admit that I worked on the basis that I may need to be registered for tax exemption at some point even though I might not generate sales to warrant it just yet. So I printed each one, signed it, scanned it back into my computer and uploaded them all into the Ingram system. To do that you click on the button marked Upload Tax Documents and upload each one in turn, assigning it to the appropriately named form.

It sounds horrendous, but it really isn't and once it is done, it is done. You can then go to your account dashboard and upload your first book. Oh, as I mentioned earlier, if you do start entering tax information then best to finish it. If you don't then you will be prompted on each and every occasion you login to finish your account setup. It's easier to get it out of the way.

I'm going to assume you have and we can now look at how you upload, prepare and publish a book through Ingram. So head to your dashboard.

Ingram Dashboard

Click on the home menu. This will give a quick snapshot of recent sales, a series of shortcut buttons to various places in the Ingram system and some help articles. To be honest, I usually bypass this screen and click on titles, where unsurprisingly, all your titles are listed.

It defaults to the last ten books you have uploaded on Ingram and will also give their published status, ISBN / EAN (an EAN is, confusingly, an International Article Number but is EAN because it used to be known as a European Article Number). The list also shows the format of the book; eBook, paperback or hardback, the author and what actions you can do, such as order copies, convert to eBook if applicable, promote through the IngramSpark catalogue and of course edit all of the details of the book. For now, you don't have any of that as you haven't uploaded your first title yet, but we'll get to that soon.

One last thing before we do. Ingram used to have a guided tour feature on their accounts and it used to be really good. It seems to have been replaced with a help centre menu item. Most of the articles you can find in there are clear and accurate and I recommend you click on each one and familiarise yourself with their system. A lot of what they talk about is covered in here, but you can't get enough information, so take the time to read the articles, or at least remember that they are there if and when you need them. For now, on the Titles Page, click the Add a New Title button.

Step 1 - Add New Title

Select to make a print book, an eBook or both. We shall be making a print book. (It says $49) more about that later.

Do you have all your files, yes, no, and no but I'll enter all the details and submit my files later. Choose that third option – even if you do have all your files. Trust me !!

What would you like to do? – If you only want to print personal copies of your book, you'd choose print only, but we want to sell your book globally and make millions, (well, make something), so you choose Print, distribute and sell my book.

Then choose continue.

Now we are on the first screen in what is a multi-step process. It asks for all the same type of information as you are now well used to providing. Title, subtitle, language, etc. Occasionally you will see "Show more fields to improve book optimization" –

click on those and fill in as much as you can.

You fill in your name as author and your imprint, all much as before. One small difference is there are two descriptions asked for, a short one totalling no more than 350 characters (not words, characters), so you need to be brief. The full description is where you can add in the one you have used previously with KDP.

The subjects can be searched for and you can enter three of them.

Audience is a new data entry that we haven't come across as yet. It should be set to trade / general (Adult) unless of course you are making a kid's book, or young adult, or if you are publishing a textbook, choose the appropriate one.

When you are ready, continue to step 2.

Step 2 - Add New Title

Trim size and other product information is the next screen. Use the drop down to choose the trim and depending on what you choose, the other options will be expanded or limited.

I am going to use the example of 8.5" x 8.5" (216mm x 216mm).

Then I can choose colour (color) or black and white. If we choose color, then we have options to choose standard on 50lb paper up to premium on 70lb paper. (The pound measure of paper is a US measurement – to see what that is in GSM, use a Google search to make the conversion). You will need to have done your homework on what you want your book to be. Then you can choose appropriately.

If it offers a duplex option, this is so you could print the inside of the cover (inside front and back covers) but be aware that KDP paperback doesn't support duplex, so you'd end up with different versions. Before we go on, just a little reminder:

Remember, if you are using the same ISBN, then the trim

size of this book and the colour of the pages and the binding, must be identical to the KDP version.

And as to binding types: for paperback fiction novels most will use perfect bound biding. Occasionally, again depending on trim size, you may be offered saddle stitched bindings. If you are not sure what these are, once more you will find either the Ingram help files or Google will be of use.

For now, the simplest way to explain it is that a perfect bound book has its pages and cover glued together at the spine with a strong yet flexible glue. The other three sides of the book are trimmed to give them clean, or 'perfect' edges.

Saddle stitch on the other hand takes folded sheets of paper, gathers them together one inside the other and then staples through the fold line with wire staples. It is commonly used for pamphlets and thin works less than 64 pages.

If you are printing a hardback book you can choose to have a cloth cover (printed or plain) with or without an additional dust jacket or you can have a laminated case which by definition won't have a dust jacket as well.

Remember, these choices will tie themselves to the ISBN on publication so be sure that you have got the binding and cover correct for your needs. This is where both the KDP and Ingram systems are extremely helpful, as you will be able to order proof copies from either before you commit to the final publishing and therefore the final assignment of ISBN.

Choose your finish, be that cloth (hardback only), matte or gloss for the cover. Then enter in the number of pages and you will see the primary cost to print the book in a range of market places.

At this point you then have a table of six different pricing points and things will get a little complicated.

Enter what you think should be a good retail price for your book in one of these lines. Let's say you put in 10.00 to the UK line. The rest of the lines will convert it to be an equivalent amount (based on whatever rates Ingram use in their backend). And at that point, there are a few things to be aware of.

Retail Price:

If pricing is not submitted for a specific market, the title will be unavailable for sale in that market. The maximum price allowed is $99.00. To set a price greater than $99.00 you would need to contact Ingram customer support. To determine retail/list price for your title:

- Consider how much you want to earn for every title sold.
- Look at the retail price (not discounted price) of titles similar to your title in genre, page count, trim size, and bind type.
- Offer your title with a list price that is considered reasonable for each market.

Wholesale Discount:

Bookshops need to have a discount, or they won't sell your book. They will demand a minimum of 40% off retail price. However, the percentage you put in here (in the Ingram interface) is NOT the discount passed on to the retailer (I know, for that would be far too easy, wouldn't it sheesh!). According to Ingram: *The wholesale discount you offer is what the distribution partners and wholesalers such as Ingram receive for selling your book and is not the discount the booksellers or consumers receive.*

So, in order for the bookseller to get 40% you would have to put your discount percentage here as 55%. There is a video link on this section of the Ingram page that explains all this in more detail.

However, be aware that whereas the KDP system recommended a minimum sales price for your book, Ingram doesn't, so it up to you to set a price that will actually make you some money. For example, if you have a recommended retail price of 19.99 (be that dollars or pounds or euros) and you set a discount of 55% then the bookseller and Ingram will share the discount based on whatever private trading arrangements they have. Suffice to say, that between the two of them, the sale price you get is going to be around 8.99, depending on page count and trim size. If the total cost for printing your book is 5.99 then the best you will make per book will be 3.00. That may appear a paltry sum for all the work that goes into writing a book, but you do not have a requirement to hold any stock, you are not required to order a minimum print run and you have no requirement to order and dispatch the books to the booksellers who order directly from Ingram. Also, I imagine if you sold 100,000 at 3.00 pounds, dollars or euros each, then you'd be fairly happy.

The thing is, if your book is big and complex and being printed as a full colour hardback then your recommended retail price is going to have to be high enough to ensure everyone can get their share. You can of course reduce the discount you offer, but the lower you go the less chance there is of online retailers stocking it. Saying that, if you set the price and a few weeks later it seems your book is invisible online, then you will know you might have got it wrong. Also, if this is a paperback and you have it on KDP as well, try to match the prices between it and IngramSpark.

Each of the US, UK, EU, Canadian and Australian markets can be set individually and then there is a global connect program for those countries where Ingram doesn't have printing facilities. You can tie these to the US pricing or set it individually if you wish.

One major point of difference with the KDP program is that Ingram prices, once set, can only be changed on a weekly basis, so be very careful in your price point selection. If you make a mistake you will be locked in for at least seven days.

Finally there is the thorny issue of returnable stock.

CAUTION!

If you choose to set your books as returnable stock, then should a bookseller order 100 of them and not sell 95, the cost for the printing of those 95 will fall to you. Big publishers can do this as they will have lots of titles out in the market place and they may get returns from all of them. Typically, when they have a palate of about 1000 books of mixed titles, they will sell these onto a reseller who will pay a minimal price but one that will cover the cost of the printing at least. That way the publisher isn't out of pocket and the reseller gets to sell discounted books at a price of their choosing. It will make them a little profit but that will be multiplied by sheer quantity of books sold.

Now, that's great for the big publishers. For you however, you need to bear in mind that unless you can find yourself a deal with a reseller, if you make your titles returnable (with the resultant books being shipped back to you) then you are likely to end up with a whole bunch of books landing back at your address. Alternatively, Ingram offer a 'Destroy Returns' option. That way you don't get any books sent back to you and you may think, 'Fair enough' but, regardless of the option, if you choose to make your titles returnable and a bookseller does indeed return them, **YOU END UP WITH THE BILL FOR PRINTING**.

That could be a significant cost, as shown in this Ingram provided example:

The book's retail/list price $20
53% wholesale discount = $9.40 wholesale price
$4.81 print cost for small paperback containing 300 pages = $4.59 in publisher compensation paid to you.

BUT

If the book is returned, Ingram charge you back the wholesale price of $9.40.

Booksellers really like returnable status and in fact most may not stock your book unless it is returnable. That has to be weighed against this issue of you receiving a potentially large bill at the end of any given month. As yet there is no way to limit the risk involved but it is one of the main issues that I am trying to have resolved through Ingram discussion groups.

For now, be aware of one last thing. If you set your books to be returnable and then decide to change your mind, IngramSpark will provide notice of the change to all distribution partners; however, booksellers will continue to have the right to return books for a period of 180 days. That could still leave you out of pocket by some margin.

This issue of returnable book status is one of the major factors that prevents Indies getting stocked by major book selling chains. It is a huge stumbling block and one that hasn't yet found a solution.

Moving on - at the right hand side of the pricing table, it will now show the Publisher's compensation. This is how much you will receive for each book sold. Except for the Australian figure, as Australia charges tax on books and so you will get less than this as you have to allow for the tax on printing costs. (I know, "sheesh"…)

Underneath that section is a series of questions, **look inside, large text, right to left**. This last one is for Arabic or other texts that read in that manner. Check it if appropriate. Don't check it for a standardised 'western' text. Large text is self-explanatory and the look inside feature is one I used to check but now I don't after reading the full terms and conditions. I didn't like them much. You should make up your own mind.

Finally on this screen, choose your print release date and on sale date. Unlike KDP you can have pre-orders set for print books on Ingram. This is excellent news as it allows your book to be marketed before its release. The publication date is the date you will make your book available to booksellers and libraries. The on-sale date is the date that you wish to release a title to be printed and delivered. Specifying an on-sale date allows you to set up a title in advance so that it becomes visible to IngramSpark's established distribution partners.

Phew! One screen but a lot of information. However, not much more to go before your book is uploaded. So click on continue and make sure to have checked the price boxes if less than 55% discount.

Step 3 - Add New Title

This is where you upload your interior and cover – both of which have to be in PDF format.

Yes you can of course use the interior file you used for KDP, but the cover template will be Ingram's own.

Click on the browse buttons for each, or drag and drop the files into their respective boxes. Once they have been uploaded, click on continue.

At which point your files will be verified for content and then…

SURPRISE!!

You will be hit for a fee.

You see Ingram's setup, conversion and access to market is not free. In fact it will cost you $49 US dollars (Sep 2022 prices) to setup a print book. There are also charges for any revisions once the first proof has been accepted. This can become expensive if you find out you have mistakes to correct and this is the main reason I recommend getting it right with KDP first if you can. With that said, there is also a way you can avoid all these expenses.

The Alliance of Independent Authors

Apart from all the other benefits being a member of the Alliance of Independent Authors (ALLi) brings, including the most phenomenal expert forums, virtual conferences, advice on everything from printing to selling book rights and the sheer camaraderie of being in a group of likeminded authors, it also bestows (as of April 2018) a discount code for IngramSpark that negates five setup and revision fees per month. That alone is normally worth the membership.

If you would like to join, feel free to use this link, which does indeed include my affiliate reference. (Donuts…):

https://www.allianceindependentauthors.org/?affid=4468

Assuming you have joined ALLi, or you have paid the IngramSpark fees, once you click on confirm you will be taken to the title submission screen. Your book will now be reviewed by the IngramSpark technical review team and within 1-2 business days, possibly 3-4 if this is the very first time you have uploaded into the system, they will get back to you with a go/no-go status. At that point you either upload new files and go through the submission process again, or you get notified that your files have been accepted and that they are pending your approval. If that is the case you are two steps away from having your book out in the world.

We shall cover those last two steps, reviewing and approving the proof shortly, but first a little about the help and support available in Ingram, the reports that you can access and how to order copies of your book.

Help

Take a look up at the Help Centre menu item. Clicking on it takes you to a screen, chock full of useful articles and assistance. If you can't find what you need, then up in the top left of the screen is a Contact Us link. This allows you to fill in a form for direct help. In my experience the Ingram helpdesk folk are superb at what they do and they endeavour to assist as quickly and as efficiently as they can. Seriously, they are very good, so don't hesitate to contact them if you have any issues with the system. Also, if your book gets caught in the maelstrom of technical review for over four days, reach out and ask them to take a look. They invariably will solve the problem.

Reports

Ah… where the IngramSpark support desks are great, to every Ying there is a Yang… Their reporting system is truly awful. Seriously, it is clunky, difficult to navigate and downright stubborn in the giving up of suitably clear information.

At first glance it does look comprehensive enough when you click on the Reports link in the top menu bar. There seems to be a whole raft of good reports waiting for you. Unfortunately, clicking on any one of them will rapidly reveal a cumbersome mechanism that only lends itself to showing multiple sales in multiple currencies if you elect to have your chosen formatted file emailed to you. Even then, when it arrives there is a ton of information which is unlikely to be of use and a small amount of data hidden within which is what you are really after.

There is no good spin to be put on these reports, other than Ingram know they are not great and hopefully 'something will be done' in the future… For now, good luck. Seriously, that's about all I have for you on this. You can use Ingram's help archive, but the best way to figure them out is quite literally to go in, select a few things and see what the report gives you.

The only other thing I can offer is that the Publisher Compensation Report is the one that tells you how much money you have made, so potentially, select a date range that you want, tick all the boxes, select the file format you want and have the reports emailed to you. I know, not the greatest piece of instruction ever given but it is difficult to teach you how to swim when you are weighed down with a hundredweight of lead… Yeah, these reports are that bad.

<u>Ordering Books</u>

On a bit more of a Ying to balance the Yang of the reports, the IngramSpark book ordering system is great. It allows you to order books in advance of the on-sale date and lets you order in US dollars, UK pounds, EU euros and Australian dollars, depending on where your final shipping address is. Each of these separate options will be printed in the printing facility best situated to meet the order's final shipping destination. You can select to have the book rush printed in a day, or more economically, printed in five days. You can select a range of postal options from overnight to standard mail delivery. All in all it is very, very good.

You access orders either from the order button next to the title on the dashboard, or through the menu item: Orders. If the latter you tick the title you want to add to the order.

Select the shipping address or add a new one, select the print location and then go to the foot of the form and select update order. That will reset the correct shipping options. Enter the number of books you wish to order and note that it will specify how many books come in a single carton. Ordering in multiples of that or less will obviously help to keep shipping costs down.

Then select your order print and shipping speeds, update the order again before submitting it. If your book is still in its pre-order phase you will have to override the on-sale date to allow the order to be processed early.

After you submit you have to confirm the payment options and then that's that. Your books are on the way. I always put an email address in so I get information on the status of the order and delivery.

The last thing that we need to look at is what happens when the files you uploaded are passed by the IngramSpark team and sent to you for approval.

Approving the Proof

When your files are approved you will be sent an email and a message will appear on your dashboard. Go to Titles and then to Pending Approval (all on the left hand menu) then when on the pending approval screen, click on the link to your book.

Sadly, this is not the KDP proofing system, so here all you will see is a download link and an email link. One opens the pdf file in a browser, the other sends an email link to you. Either way, you need to open the file and scroll down through it, checking the layout of the cover and the interior file. Be particular in your examination. If it is as you expected, you can approve it. However, on the proof approval screen it gives you a number of options:

- You approve this title for distribution into the sales channels.
- You approve this title but withhold from distribution into the sales channels.
- You do not approve this title. Select a reason from the list below:
- You have revised content to upload.

- You reject the proof and request further review. Please provide your rejection notes in the box below.

As I strongly urged you in the KDP proofing process, once again I strongly urge you here, order a physical, printed proof copy from Ingram before you release your masterpiece into the world. The option to approve but withhold allows you to have complete confidence that you can order a proof version without any risk of your book making its way into the world until after you have assessed it in physical form. Once you are sure, you can return to the title status and release it into the sales channels. To do this last step, return to your title page, on the right hand side button, choose the drop down and select Enable Distribution. Follow the prompts and that's that! You will now have published your paperback and eBook to IngramSpark, Draft2Digital and Kindle Direct Publishing (in two formats). You are an Indie author.

Congratulations!!

9

Formatting for Print and eBook

As with most things in life there are, at the very least, six ways to accomplish anything. Formatting your Word document for use as both a 'physical' book and an eBook can be managed in all manner of ways. You may be a keyboard wizard, or witch, scurrying away with 'fantastical' word processing programs, like Scrivener. You may handwrite your manuscript or type it in basic fonts and send it to a third-party scribing and formatting service. You may dictate it and your word processing conversion software does all the hard work for you. All of these and more are terrific ways of getting your document formatted.

Especially the sending it to a ***third-party service*** because I run one of those and reformatting documents into paperback, hardback and eBook formats is a bread-and-butter offering that keeps me in those donuts I mentioned earlier.

However, if like the vast majority of people, you are a mere two-finger-typist mortal, who continues to plough lonely furrows with that bastion of word processing software, the mighty Microsoft® Word, then there is no need for anyone else to become involved in your formatting. You can do it yourself. Seriously. It's actually quite simple once you have mastered some straightforward concepts.

Now, I've mentioned that in a former life I was an accredited trainer of all things Microsoft and the biggest revelation to me was how poorly prepared people were when their companies gave them a PC and expected them to 'get on with it'.

I mean, you wouldn't let a welder just weld, but most companies let an administrator wield their way through Word. Normally woefully.

Thankfully, it needn't be that way. To master the techniques that allow you to rapidly and consistently format a document is a simple matter of using things that expert programmers have already built into Word. Sadly, so few even know these things exist, let alone how to use them, but this chapter will change that for you, albeit in a fairly brisk way.

All you need to do is read along, however, if you had a Word document open on your computer then you could follow along as well and that would be even better. Caution though!! Make sure you save a copy of it before you start messing about – just in case.

So, we want to format a Word document such that it sails through the approval process for Amazon's and IngramSpark's systems as well as D2D. That means you are going to need two versions. The easiest way to manage this is for you to write your book. Finish your manuscript. It doesn't matter what format it is in. You will have it all finished, edited and 'put to bed'. Then you are going to format an eBook version and a Print version. So save your manuscript out twice: eBook Master and Print Master.

Note: All the following screens refer to

Microsoft Word Home Office 2013

If you are using a different version and cannot find the commands mentioned, use the help function in Word.

First - Learn to view your document correctly

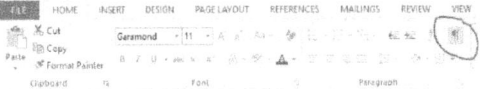

First things first. To use Word effectively, you need to see the formatting marks, so turn them on. Yes, really! That little backwards facing **P** up on the Ribbon, under the **home** tab in the **paragraph** group. It's called the **'Show/Hide'** command. Turn it on. You need to know where your paragraph marks are. Where the extra spaces are, where the tabs are and where the page breaks are – so use the thing that shows you them all. You also need to see the **ruler** and your **navigation** pane – so go to the Ribbon, select the **view** tab and turn those both on in the **show** group.

Trim Size - Again

Great news. The layout of an eBook does not give a jot about what size your page is set to. Neither does it care what your margins are set at. It is a free flowing formatted document file and wants the explicit ability to resize for whatever electronic device it is being shown on. Therefore, the page needs to be resizable automatically. The only page breaks it cares about are at the start of a new chapter, so you will of course keep these in your document, but you have no need of section breaks, headers, footers, page numbers or anything else that will curtail this free flow. You also have no need of automatic hyphenation (so if you have added it, it can be taken off). If you don't know what that is, do not fret, we shall come to it soon enough.

That said, if you put all of those things in as you were typing your manuscript then of course, make sure you save a copy of the Word document containing them as your 'Print Master' file.

Clear enough? Your eBook master can be stripped of all blank pages, all section breaks, all headers, all footers (including page numbers) all hyphenation. The size of it as a 'page size' is irrelevant.

However… You will need to set your trim size and page breaks and section breaks in your Print file. As discussed at length in a previous chapter, to choose what size of book you want, pick a book you like, measure it and use these dimensions to select and download a template document from KDP. You will now use that as your baseline.

Downloading a template is by far the preferred way to set your page size up as it will also set up your margins for you. But in case you don't have that luxury you will need to go to **page layout** on the Ribbon of your Word document and select **size**. Then select **more paper sizes** – use the drop down box to select **custom size** and type in the proper width and length in the respective boxes. Make certain you apply the size change to the whole document by selecting that option from the lower dropdown box.

Once your page size is set you will need to set your margins. Now, a printed book is a strange beast when it comes to margins. Depending on the size and critically, the number of pages and therefore the 'thickness' of the book, your margins will vary. Also, they need to be offset and mirrored – as in, imagine having a book open in front of you. The inner margin on the left-hand page and the inner margin on the right-hand page need to be the same, but the inner on the left is the right-hand margin and the inner on the right is the left-hand margin – get it? The 'outer' margins are different to the inner, but have to be the same throughout. Luckily, Word does all of this for you in one simple dialogue box. Phew! Just go to page layout on the Ribbon, select **margins** and then, at the bottom of the options select **custom margins**. Enter in the appropriate margin widths for your trim size. If you don't know what these are you will have to search the Internet for the appropriate information. Make sure you select **mirror margins** and apply the settings to the whole document. Now, hopefully you can see why a downloaded preformatted template is such a good idea.

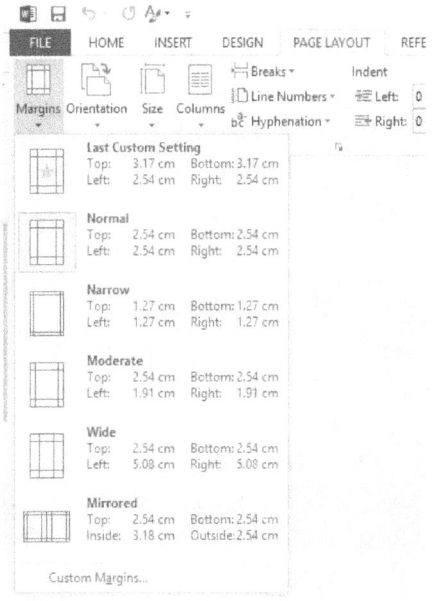

Section Breaks

Your eBook doesn't need these. Your Print file does. Reason being, in some of your book you will want to have page numbers in the footer (or header if you want to be trendy) but in other parts of the book, like the title and copyright pages, you won't want numbers. You will / may also want to add the author's name in to the header on top of the even (or odd) pages and the chapter, or book title on the opposing page header.

To do all of these 'fiddly' things, you need to have section breaks in your document. Again, the good news is, Word makes it easy. Simply put your cursor at the foot of a page, select **Page Layout** and on the drop down next to the word **Breaks**, you get options for **'Section Break – Next Page'**. Choose it and Word will not only put in a section break, but it will add a new page as well. Viola! You have added a new section to your document. You can now set the headers and footers in this section to be different from the other sections by unclicking **'Link to Previous'**. That is a first step to mastering your headers and footers.

Master your Headers and Footers.

Again, not needed or wanted in an eBook, but most definitely wanted in a printed book. You need page numbers in a paperback or hardback. DO NOT add them manually. Double click into your footer and position your cursor where you want your page number to appear. You'll see that the **Design Tab** has appeared on the Ribbon. Select **Page Number** from the **Header & Footer** group. Choose **Current Position** and then put in the page number format you want. Oh and tick **Different Odd & Even Pages** in the **Options** group on the design tab as you'll need that too.

Well, you will if you want to have a different layout to the odd and even pages. You may wish to have this if you position your page number at the 'outside' of each page. Obviously the odd numbered pages will have the number set to the right and the even numbered pages will have it set to the left. Likewise if you want the author's name on the top of the right hand side page and the title of the book on the left hand side you will have to set up different odd and even headers. This single check in the different odd and even pages makes this possible.

Chapter Headings and Scene Breaks

Ah ha. At last. A bit that can be put into both eBook and Print. However, your eBook master file is better off with no quirky fonts or weird inclusions. A plainer, more easily readable file is what you are after for eBooks. You can have weird and unusual drop caps at the start of each chapter of your Print book, but eBooks don't really care for the wild and wacky. In fact the KDP conversion process will simply 'dumb down' any fonts it doesn't like. So, for an eBook, keep it simple. You can be as fancy as you like in a printed version.

Your chapter headings in a printed book can be creative and artistic and, as long as you save the document out properly, 'What you see is what you will get' from KDP and Ingram. So, use drop caps and fiddly, twirly lines and whatever else you want, but please be consistent.

Ensure each and every chapter begins by looking the same. Make especially sure that the device you use for a scene break, be it three *** or a complex line with diamonds and geometrics or a fleur-de-lys has consistent spacing around it. There is nothing more jarring to the reader's eye than inconsistent layout features.

Styles

This is potentially the greatest time saving invention in Microsoft® Word. Sadly, it also a feature that so very few people know about or use.

Each heading, each paragraph, each inclusion in your manuscript should be assigned a style. This is the same for both eBooks and Print. We can use the built-in styles or we can make our own. Either way they are powerful ways of rapidly and consistently changing the format of your whole book with minimal effort.

If you have never used them, they are on the **home** tab of the Ribbon and fill the whole middle section across to the right hand side. There is also a small arrow dropdown on the far right that, when accessed, will allow you to create your own style. We will use a built-in style for the chapter headings and a self-made one for paragraphs.

One small note before we begin. A printed book doesn't actually need a chapter heading, although of course most have them. An eBook normally absolutely requires them and will also need a Table of Contents to allow readers to navigate through the book quickly. On absolutely **NO ACCOUNT** ever put your Table of Contents in manually. It is a most flawed way of doing it. If you use styles properly the Table of Contents is a doddle to insert.

Right then!! Styles.

The key to this is to make everything as easy as possible. So, most books will have a non-indented paragraph style for the start of a chapter or the start of the text after a line break. It would look like this:

A paragraph after a line break or at the start of a chapter. It may be one line long, it may be many lines long. It may be one sentence or many sentences. What is important is that it is not indented. To make your use of styles easy, simply format that first paragraph exactly how you want it. No indent, font size and style set as you wish it to be. For example, the paragraph you are reading now is set to have no first line indent, the font is set as black, Garamond 11 and the whole paragraph is fully justified. Having set my paragraph to be what I want, I am now going to set it as a style. To do that, select the whole of the paragraph (easiest way to do this is to click on it three times rapidly with your left hand mouse key). Once selected, go up to the **styles** group on the Ribbon and select the small dropdown arrow to the right of the main box.

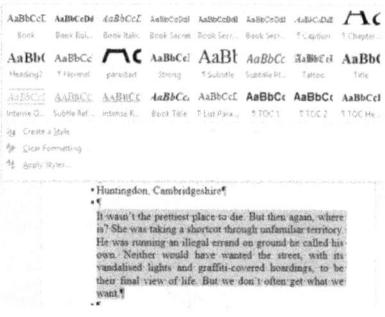

Select **Create a Style** and give it a name. I tend to number mine to keep them in order so I would call this one 1.0 First Para.

Then I would do the same with the next paragraph in my manuscript, which, like this one you are currently reading, has a first line indent that is set to .2 of an inch. Once again I make sure it is as I want it, select the whole paragraph, click on the dropdown arrow and **create a style**. This one I might call 2.0 Main Body. You only need these two usually.

Once I have both of these I can apply them to every single paragraph as appropriate in my document.

For example, I would go to the first paragraph in each chapter, click into it, (you don't need to select it, just click anywhere in the paragraph) then click on the style **1.0 First Para** up in the Ribbon. That automatically sets it as the paragraph's style. Ideally you would do this as you are writing your manuscript but it can be done retrospectively extremely quickly. You then set all your indented paragraphs to be 2.0 Main Body.

Why on earth would you or should you bother? Well, you see you can also modify styles. You right hand mouse click over the name of the style and you can see it says **modify**. Selecting that allows you to alter everything about it from font to spacing to colour if you wanted. One single modification to that style will cascade through every single paragraph that has the style applied. It means you can change your whole document layout in seconds. Styles are the key to efficient and consistent formatting of Word documents.

Using the Built-In Heading Styles

Having created our own styles, we also want to use some of the built-in styles. However, we want them to reflect what we want, not what they think we want. In the styles group on the Ribbon you should see styles called Heading 1, Heading 2 and Heading 3. These are exactly what we want to use for making an automatic Table of Contents. They are also excellent in making sure all the headings throughout our manuscript are consistent. However, the settings they come with are usually completely wrong for what we want. Sooooo… we're going to use them but make them work for us.

To begin, set your chapter heading to be exactly as you want it. Perhaps it will look something like this:

Chapter 8

Having set it, in this case to be centred, Garamond, bold, italicised, black text at font size 18, I can now select all of it, and then, with it highlighted, go to the Ribbon, find Heading 1 and **RIGHT HAND CLICK** on the style. Select the option that says, **Update Heading 1 to Match Selection.** You have now made the built-in style Heading 1 be centred, Garamond, bold, italicised, black text at font size 18. You have also ensured that it has now appeared in the navigation pane over on the left of your screen which means you can quickly navigate through your document by clicking on it over there.

Now all you have to do is set each chapter heading to be that style. Just go and find the next heading, highlight it then apply the Heading 1 style to it by left hand clicking on the style.

Soon, all your chapter headings will look the same and they will be in the navigation pane. They will also be ripe for turning into a Table of Contents, but we'll look at that a bit later.

You can also add other styles to Heading 2 and Heading 3. For example, in this book I use Heading 1 for the chapter number, Heading 2 for the title of the chapter and Heading 3 for the sub-titles throughout the chapters.

Before we move on, in your Print version of your book, select **Page Layout** on the Ribbon. Then select **Hyphenation automatic**. That will ensure the paragraph text wraps properly at the end of every line. This is usual in all books bar those meant for young children. It will automatically add a hyphen into a word that has fallen at the end of a line. Now that I have drawn your attention to it you may think this is weird and unusual, but trust me. If you are reading the printed version of this book then you are reading a paragraph with an automatically placed hyphen in its first line and you probably didn't even notice. Go and take any book from your book shelf and look through it. Unless it is book for early readers, automatic hyphens probably appear throughout. For eBooks, turn this option off. They don't need it.

Insert your own Hyperlinks

What you might want in an eBook are hyperlinks. If your reading device is connected to the Internet then you can add in links to other webpages, review sites, your own email (if you want people to be able to contact you), your social media sites and perhaps most important of all, the sales pages of your books.

To add a link, copy the web address you want to direct people to, then highlight the text within your file that you want to act as the link. Right hand click and select **hyperlink**. Paste the web address into the box that asks for the address or click the 'Email Address' button and enter the details to add an email.

If you are on the eBook version of this book, the link below is a text hyperlink that when clicked, will send me an email.

Send me an email

Insert a Hyperlinked Table of Contents.

All eBooks and some printed books will need a Table of Contents. If you have used the in-built Word headings (Heading 1, 2 and 3) then inserting a Table of Contents is a simple matter of going to an empty page at the start of your document, somewhere after the title page, clicking on the **Reference Tab** in the Ribbon, clicking on the Table of Contents and selecting Custom Table of Contents.

For an eBook, you should turn off page numbers and select hyperlinks. For a print book, leave page numbers on. If you want to you can modify all sorts of layouts and fonts to your heart's content, or you can click OK and that is that! Seriously. If you have used those Headings 1, 2 and 3 then your Table of Contents is done.

It is quick and automatic and saves you an awful lot of work.

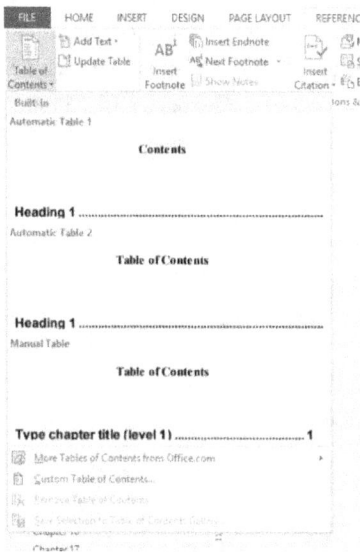

Save your document as a PDF-A

KDP for print will take your interior files as a Word document. It will convert the file into their required format, however, the bottom page margin can be a bit hit and miss and occasionally, if you have a page that is 'full' of text, KDP can occasionally 'throw' the last line onto the next page so that you end up with what is often called an orphan line. You don't want orphan lines, not least because they can add an extra page to your book for no good reason and every page increases the printing costs. IngramSpark won't accept a raw Word file. Both KDP and Ingram Spark will accept PDF-A formatted files.

This type of PDF fixes the layout and page breaks by locking the format in. So, save yourself time and effort by uploading the same interior file, PDF-A format to both IngramSpark and KDP. But, I hear you cry, (well, muffled whimpers probably) 'How do I make a PDF-A?'

Simple. In your Print master document, go to the **File** menu in Word, choose **Save As**, navigate to where you want your document to be saved and save it first as a standard Word document. This is and always will be your master file. Then, go back to **Save As**, navigate to the same folder and this time, select the drop-down under the filename and select **PDF**.

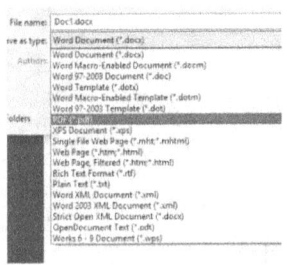

Once you have done that you will see a small button called **Options** has appeared. Click on it and you will get an Options dialogue box.

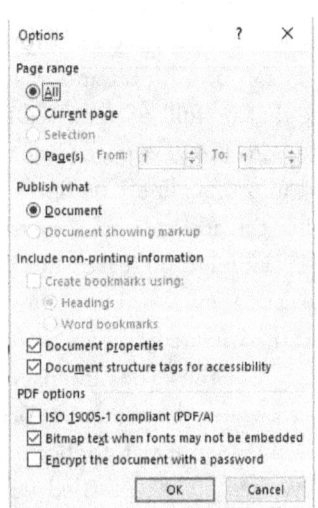

Now, check the option that says **ISO 19005-1 compliant (PDF/A)**. Once checked, leave the rest of the default options as they are, click **OK**, check you have the filename you want and then click **save**. That's it. Upload that PDF file into KDP and IngramSpark and you are done.

For your eBook version all you have to do is save the Word version of your book as this is what we'll use for uploading to KDP and for converting through to an ePub file for D2D (more of which in the next chapter).

Obviously, there are a few other things you have to do before you upload anything to anywhere. Things like, finish your book, get it professionally edited, get a professional cover designed (including a great spine), sort out your front and end matter (copyright pages, dedication pages, acknowledgement pages, about the author pages, also by pages etc. If you really want to think about front and end matter, take a look at the pages in this book that appear before the first chapter and after the last one. See, not rocket science…).

You'll also want to sort out your ISBNs of course, but other than those minor issues, if you do the tips above, you will be well on your way.

10

Using Calibre to make your ePub

To make your own ePub document that you can upload to D2D, download a shareware program called Calibre from:

https://calibre-eBook.com/

Shareware means you can download it and use it for free, but they would like you to contribute a donation if you think it is a good piece of software. It is a good piece of software.

Once downloaded and installed on your computer, click on **Add Books** in the top left of the screen. Browse to the Word document that you have now formatted for eBook, as in your master eBook file that doesn't have page numbers, section breaks, extra blank pages and that does have consistently styled chapter headings and an automatically inserted Table of Contents. Then click to upload it into Calibre.

Once the upload is finished click on **Edit Metadata**. Fill in the correct title of your book, the author name and then click the green arrows next to those boxes. In the middle of the screen browse for your cover art and upload it.

Fill in the tags, (as in Crime or Science Fiction or whatever other tags you think are pertinent). Fill in the date you are uploading the file into Calibre and the planned publication date of the book. Enter the publishers name (probably your own name or the Imprint you are using). Choose the book's language. Add the ePub ISBN in to the identifiers box. Then in the bottom right click on **OK** and close the window.

Once that is complete click on **Convert Books**. Set the input format in the top left to be DOCX. Set the output format in the top right to be EPUB. On the menu to the left, select **Structure Detection**. Then, in the main screen, where it says **Chapter Mark**, select that to be **None**.

Again on the left, select Table of Contents. Ensure 'Do not add detected chapters to the Table of Contents' is checked. Also check 'Manually fine-tune the ToC after conversion is completed'.

Click **OK**.

Your Word document will be converted into an ePub. Once it is ready the Table of Contents will be displayed for you to verify. If correct, click OK and let the conversion complete. If it isn't correct either manually change it or let the conversion complete, return to your master Word document and reset your headings to be appropriate. Insert your automatic Table of Contents again. The return to Calibre and under **Add Books**, select add files to selected book record. That will overwrite the old Word document with your latest version. Then repeat the conversion process.

Once you have a clean conversion, on the right hand side of the screen, under your cover art is a link that says **Path: Click to Open**. Click it and copy the ePub file that is there. Place it somewhere you can find it on your computer. This is the ePub file you will now use to upload to D2D.

At this point you will have four files.

1. A master Word document formatted for Print.
2. A 'PDF-A' formatted file saved from the master Print file. This PDF-A is what you will use to upload into KDP and IngramSpark.
3. A master Word document formatted for eBook. You will upload this file directly into KDP.
4. An ePub. You will upload this file to D2D.

Congratulations. If you also have your cover files, then you have all the files you need to be an Indie author.

11

Audio Books

Ah, the dulcet tones of Stephen Fry reading out your book. Stuff that dreams are made of. Also stuff that I would imagine (and I have no proof) might cost a considerable penny or two.

Stephen 'National Treasure' Fry, I imagine, might be a bit expensive to hire for voice actor work. However, if you can perhaps aim slightly lower on the actor stratosphere, then audio books can be achieved for less than you may think.

In fact, if you have written a factual book, or indeed, your own biography or memoir, you can record it yourself. All you need is a decent microphone, a relatively soundproof or sound neutral environment and software such as Audacity ™. At that point you would be set to go. However, if your book has a requirement for different character voices, perhaps different accents, tone, pace, pathos etc, then you will probably want to get a professional voice actor. They usually cost money, but not always as much as you might think.

In fact, were you to use a popular method, you could achieve it for almost nothing, but (for various reasons, mainly to do with rights ownership) I do not recommend it. Having said that, I still need to tell you about it.

Amazon's very own, ACX

A small recap from Chapter 3. D2D have a hook-up / tie-in with Findaway Voices, but when I thought about making an audio book, I went to the big player in the marketplace first: Amazon's ACX.

They have actors looking to read books and if you go on there as an author looking for an actor, ACX will do the "matchmaking" and you can produce an audio book for nothing. Except you get nothing for nothing and so there are a few things to be aware of, like royalty rates and rights attribution and length of those rights deals (which used to be set to 7-years of exclusivity with ACX). However, the major elephant in the room for me being in Australia was that ACX don't (as of September 2022) allow you to have an ACX account if you live here. In fact, ACX only operate in a few countries and unless I fancied pretending not to be in Australia, that was that for me.

I have already mentioned about the 'Audiblegate Scandal' so I shan't repeat it all again, but given all of those circumstances, I had to find another way to make my audio books.

What I chose was quite simple. Contact voice agencies, identify some actors that I thought might be a good fit. Send an initial email to say, this is the project, I would like you to submit a small audition piece and, crucially as I believe it set the expectations, I indicated the budget I had to work with.

I got some actors that said no. I got some that said yes and sent back their first audition piece. I whittled them down to a shortlist, invited some to do a second short reading and from that I selected the voice I wanted. We signed contracts and went from there. All of which seems straightforward, but of course there's a bit more to it than that.

Let's talk about exactly what you might be getting for your

money. Audio books are costed in a number of ways and it depends on the voice talent you hire. I have worked with all three types and I'll expand on which is easier, and what you do with the completed files later. For now though, you have these options:

1. The actor has their own recording studio and technical skills so that the file you get back is complete and finished. The editing, the finished audio levels, the final mastering of the file and the fulfilment of standards for an audio book are done and you only have to upload it to be ready to release it.

2. The actor has their own recording studio and they provide all editing of the file so that what you get back is a complete recording, but you need to have the audio mastered to be fit for upload and release.

3. The actor records the file but all their outtakes, rework attempts and clicks, bumps, whistles and whatever else was recorded are also left in. You need to do all the editing to get the final audio and then have it mastered fit for publication.

4. And just for completeness, Option 4 – you have recorded it all yourself and you know all about sound levels and mastering and so you have all the files in the right format at the right specifications and you are ready to upload. If that's the case, skip down to 'Publishing Audio Books'.

You may think that of the "hiring talent options", option 3 would be the cheapest, but that is not necessarily so, as the actor doing the basic recording might well be more expensive in the first place. They may be so in demand that this is all they do, record the book. Someone else can sort out the editing and mastering.

Option 1, is great. You pay the money and you get a finished file. Nothing else to be done. Well, almost. You still have to listen to every single file and read along with your actual book. If there is a mistake, you note it down and send it back to the actor to redo. This process is important. You are the last arbiter of quality control and if you are intending to have an unabridged version of your book, then it needs to match exactly.

In option 2, you pay the money, get the files and after doing the initial quality check, you then get a sound engineer. Now, when I used this method, I went to (and I wouldn't usually recommend it) but this is the exception to prove "my rule" – I went on to Fivrr and found myself a great audio engineer. His name is Jamie and he is superb. I passed on the files, he did what he does and I got them back, ready to upload for publication. If you want to reach out to him for your own projects, contact him at:

Jamie-247@hotmail.co.uk

Option 3, cost me a lot of time and quite a bit of expense in getting decent software, (and learning how to use it) but then I had it and in the long-term it didn't seem so bad.

First I bought Audacity, the audio editor. As I got each file (and I specifically asked for each chapter to be recorded as a separate file, but even that didn't work and I sometimes got three or four chapters all in one file, which I then had to divide up).

I loaded it into Audacity and armed with a copy of my book I went through and cut out all the outtakes and misreads. Once I had a collated, complete and coherent version, I went back through and took out any clicks and whirs and whatever else was in it that shouldn't have been. Then I tried to master the audio, but in the end I gave up and passed it on to Jamie as well. But I had to do that initial edit, as I obviously knew what my books should sound like. Now, I have no doubt I could have paid Jamie to do that bit too, but I was on a budget.

Ultimately, option 1 (the complete finished files) are charged at what is called PFH, per finished hour. They will include the voice talent and their studio skills. Option 2, is also charged PFH, but without the mastering and so you have to factor those additional costs in. Option 3 involves a lot more post recording work to be done by yourself (or paid for) and an actor that is paid (usually a day-rate) just to complete the read.

<u>Voice Talent</u>

I used three principal ways of finding voice talent.

- I logged into ACX and looked at the voice talent they had on there. Then I contacted the ones I wanted to and asked if they would be interested in a fee-based commission outside of ACX. Of the ones I asked, half said yes.
- I contacted emVoices (Australian-based) and sent them an email.

    https://www.emvoices.com.au/

- And finally, I contacted Sue Terry Voices.

    (https://www.sueterryvoices.com/)

If you visit that last site, you will be blown away at the talent they have on their books and who can be hired for a fee that will not price you out of the game. However, I hadn't really a clue how it all worked when I first made contact and so I started with a simple email to Sue Terry and to emVoices, laying out who I was and what I wanted and what voice talent I was interested in.

The reply was straightforward and simple. This is the specification of finished file you will get from us and these actors will charge £xx per day and these ones will charge £xx per day.

From there I sent in audition pieces, (note that some higher-end talent won't do an audition, as you know what you will be getting with them). For those that will do auditions, I was always conscious that for an actor to do a read through it can be time consuming and they aren't getting paid for an audition sample, so I kept it to an absolute minimum length, while allowing me to make a decision on it. That meant choosing a passage that included the principle characters, as if they couldn't nail them then it wouldn't work.

To accompany the piece, I sent along dialogue notes or direction about accents needed or other specifics, which brings me on to the preparation you need to do.

Preparation

To prepare the notes for audition and later, to prepare the voice talent for the whole reading, I went through the book, page by page and noted down every single character that appeared in the book and who had a "speaking part". Then I made notes on them along the lines of:

Kara Wright
female - mid 30s, west-country accent, former military.
Charles Randal (Chaz)
male - mid 30s, Manchester, former military.

I gave minimal direction with regard to how I wanted the book to sound. Yes, I did make notes if there were certain key areas I wanted in a certain way, but overall, I left it up to the actors. They did not need an amateur "wannabe director" interfering with what they did for a living. That said, if they did record it incorrectly, I would do a pick up on the first listen and report back. Most will do an initial read of a chapter or two and allow you to give direction on it and from there they will look after it. However, do not be afraid to go back to them if they have made a mistake. Even top-end voice talent are happy to correct actual errors, such as, "You read it as Hue (rhyming with phew) but it should be pronounced 'way'" If it was really difficult (as in the correct pronunciation of that Vietnamese town) I'd find a YouTube clip of someone saying it with the correct pronunciation, or record it myself and send it as a voicemail.

Also, you have to give them a time stamp as to where in the recording the error occurred, so they can listen back and put it in context. It ends up looking something like this:

Time - 11:34 - You read "savage" should be "ravage"

Some voice actors will have their own templated feedback forms; use theirs and make things as easy as possible.

Publishing Audio Books

There are, as usual, many ways to publish your audio book. Personally, as I mentioned in Chapter 3 - I went with Findaway Voices. Now, Findaway also offer voice talent on their system and you can ask their talent to audition. However, I found their prices to be more expensive than what I could get by approaching talent directly. I don't know why that is, it was just my experience. It may not always be the case. So make sure to check for yourself.

The registration process for a Findaway Voices account is as you would expect. Sign up, open the account, input all your details (very similar to D2D or KDP), and then accept their distribution agreements. If you read and agree to them, obviously.

Having not used Findaway for auditions or selection of a narrator, I merely wished to use them to host audio books I had completed elsewhere and so I clicked on the green button to start a **+NEW PROJECT**. From there I chose to sell an existing audiobook. It is, as they state on their website, completely free to upload and distribute. (They take a cut of sales, obviously).

The next set of screens will look very similar to those you have seen before on KDP or D2D –title, name , contributors, ISBN, description etc etc.

However, there are a few differences. You will be the author, but the voice talent will also be added as a contributor. Is the book abridged or unabridged? (Is it the full text, or have you left bits out (perhaps a text book, but you have left out the tables and indexes and appendices etc, or you have truncated down a novel).

It also asks for a retail ISBN and a library ISBN. They do not have to be different and if I am honest, I do not know why they would be… However, you do need to enter an ISBN and this will be the audio book's own ISBN. Different to print or eBook as it is a different format.

There is a street date and a release date, which for a new book will be the same (there are explanatory notes on Findaway for each of these if you need to know what they are).

Then you have copyright dates which can be different. My book was originally written in 2015, so the 'source' copyright was 2015 and the audio was set to 2020.

At the foot of the form Findaway recommend a cost based on finished hour length of your book. Don't vary too much from their recommendations as they are using industry averages, but ultimately you can set whatever price you like.

Then you go to the screen where you will upload all your completed files. Give each file a title and remember you will need to have recorded opening and closing titles and a retail sample. If you are not sure what these should sound like, listen to any audio book that you have previously bought. It should sound like them. I know that may sound trite, but it's the truth. Listen to one and you will know what is needed. Why reinvent the wheel?

Once you review the chapter titles, then you can choose who to distribute to. And here we come to the crunch. I chose to distribute to all 46 channels (September 2022) but as I said in Chapter 3, audio book royalties are **A JOKE**. In my humble opinion, they are the worst return on investment I have ever come across. If my book is downloaded by a subscriber to Amazon's Audible, occasionally (depending on subscription rates and location, what day of the week it is and whether oysters are in season – I may be exaggerating slightly, but seriously, I am truly at a loss as to what actually constitutes it) I may only get 26cents per download. Conversely, if the same book is downloaded via Authors Direct, I make almost $6.00. The average is about $2.00 for a book where the retailer is making in excess of $15.00 per sale.

It is hardly inspiring and of course, as Audible is the largest supplier of audio books in the world, you don't really have a choice of not using them. Yet, with that all said and done, you will have an audio version of your book out there, read by a professional (or yourself) and it gives you another income stream, even if it is modest.

Of course, the key is to get people to buy your audio books from Authors Direct, and so it would be remiss of me not to point you there:

https://shop.authors-direct.com/collections/leschenault-press

And yes, I did indeed get Gemma Whelan from *Game of Thrones* fame to read my crime books (well, the first three so far) and it was a delight to be able to work with someone with such a mastery of accents and diction.

12

Other Considerations

Legal Deposit

I have to admit, I love libraries. Ever since I was a little boy and got taken to my local one each and every week. I think they are the mainstay and the mark of a civilised society.

Seriously, I'm not even being too over-reaching in their praise. With a purpose in life to allow anyone, poor or rich access to information, entertainment and ultimately the best of all the accumulated knowledge and literature on the planet, I think they are something to be in awe of. I am and always will be thrilled to see a vibrant library at the heart of a community.

With that in mind, imagine my thrill, surprise, delight and absolute amazement to discover that being an Indie Published Author, I was legally required to deposit a copy of my book in the Australian National Library in Canberra. It got even better when I discovered the Library of Western Australia were also entitled to have one deposited for their archives.

Turns out this thing called Legal Deposit is a statutory provision requiring publishers (and remember, if you are doing this yourself, you are your own publisher) to deposit copies of their publications in a nominated collecting institute. The Legal Deposit system ensures that the works of authors and publishers will be preserved for present and future generations and is applicable in all countries. Of course, you are only subject to the countries that you either publish in or are a citizen of. (Unless you are publishing other writer's works too and then the rules change a little – but you'd have to look those up for yourself at that point).

As I live in Australia and specifically Western Australia (WA), I was obliged to contribute to their collections. Although as you've probably figured, I didn't take it as an obligation, more a privilege.

The idea behind all this is, according to the WA Library website, that the collections formed through Legal Deposit provide a valuable resource for research into all aspects of Western Australian life: its history and culture including artistic, commercial, technical and scientific endeavour.

It is also a requirement for all Australian publications to be deposited with the National Library of Australia. I dutifully sent my copy off to Canberra and took one copy up to the WA State Library in Perth. The lady there said they really would like two copies, one for the archive and one for the shelf. I happily handed them over.

I then discovered that being originally from Northern Ireland, I could also have my books Legally Deposited in the UK. That meant a copy in the British Library and the Cambridge Library, the Bodleian Library, the National Library of Scotland in Edinburgh, the National Library of Wales in Cardiff and by a quirk of the British system, Trinity Library, Dublin.

I was a bit put out that the Northern Irish Library System wasn't included, but a quick email told me that they had a voluntary deposit system operating out of the main Belfast Library. I happily donated my books to all of them and even threw in a couple for the privately owned Linen Hall Library in Belfast. After I was done, I quite seriously thought, "You know what, I could die happy right now. My books are in the library."

You can also donate two copies to the Library of Congress in the USA, especially if you are getting them printed over there through Ingram or KDP.

Now, bear in mind these are copies you have to pay for and donate. It was quite the revelation to me to find out that there are wholesale suppliers of books to libraries in general (not the national archives) and so it was a very pleasant surprise when I contacted them and they issued an order for copies. Real sales, to libraries. Even better.

You will have similar specialist suppliers to the libraries in your country. Either Google it, or simpler still, go into your local library and ask them who it is. You can also enquire about Public Lending Rights and how you get paid through the national systems in your respective country. Yes, in most countries, if you have books supplied to libraries and they are being loaned out, you will receive a payout at the end of the year – but only if you have registered for and claimed the money.

Whilst you are in your local library, ask them if they would like to host a book launch event for you, their local author. Don't ask, don't get.

Selling into Bookstores

I've already mentioned that without making returns available through IngramSpark you are unlikely to make the break into bookshops. This is true. However, you can sell your book through bookshops if you are prepared to get out and meet your local bookseller.

It does somewhat mean you are potentially restricted in geographical terms, but if you are willing to make the effort you can reap the rewards. All I can offer is my experience. It is really a tale of two shops. It starts out with a factually correct statement, 'ish…

I was the No.1 bestselling crime fiction writer of 2015.

I was. That is true. Well, I mean the whole statement would end with:

In one bookshop, in one town, in Australia.

Yeah, I know… it rather takes the shine off it doesn't it? But the fact remains.

Thing is, the shop in question is in a small but busy tourist-town which has three bookshops. One is a national chain, one is prominent on the main street and one is tucked away up a discreet, yet vibrant, little shopping 'lane'.

Back in early 2015 I had two titles on release and decided I would try to get them stocked in this nearby tourist haven. I dismissed the national chain as 'too hard' and so that left two shops to be considered. I approached the best situated of them. It was a mix of traditional bookshop and tourist ware, all the better to attract the passing trade, I thought. They were more than happy to take both of my titles (on consignment naturally, which means you give them over for no money and if and when they sell, you divide the profits in whatever manner you have agreed). I went home feeling pleased.

Six months later, in early October 2015, they had sold one of one and two of the other. I was saddened. Then a friend asked if I had tried the third bookshop. I dropped in and offered them my two titles. At this point we need to discuss…

The Face!

It is that sceptical look of 'Oh, here we go again…' from the poor bookshop owner who thinks, "Another waste of time from a self-published author."

You can't really blame them given that tidal wave of less than great publishing that exploded after PoD took off and that we have already touched on at the start of this book. If the book is dross it won't sell and if it won't sell it is taking up space on a shelf that could be filled with one that might. Book selling is a business. It isn't a gentle hobby for the fun of it. Booksellers are entitled to choose what they stock.

Anyway, you brave their face and hand your book or books over. That's what I did and I was told, unlike the first shop, that they wouldn't be accepting them straight away. Rather, they said they'd read them and get back to me. I went home and waited.

Two weeks later I rang to check on progress. I was told, "Sorry, haven't had a chance to read them yet." I figured they probably never would. Ah well… That was that. I figure ask once, follow up once and then leave it. Otherwise it is a bit… uncomfortable… awkward… you know what I mean?

Two weeks after that, the owner phoned me. She and her husband had read both my books and loved them. They'd be happy to stock them. So happy, that their initial order was twice that of any other shop I had been stocked in. I delivered the first batch myself and struck up a long and wandering conversation with the owners. They learnt about me, I learnt about them.

So it was, that within the last quarter of 2015 they sold so many of my novels that I outperformed every other author on their shelves, including Galbraith, Connolly, Child, et al. I not only caught up with their year-to-date totals, but surpassed them. I was thrilled, but also slightly confused. What on earth had happened and why was there such a disparity with the first shop, separated as it was by only a few hundred metres?

On reflection, the answer was simple enough. The shop on the main street sold books. As a commodity. Like tourist gifts and greeting cards. The product sat on a shelf and waited to be chosen. That works. Of course it does. If you are a known name.

The second shop is owned and staffed by bibliophiles, book lovers, book readers, book geeks. Lovely ones, but definitely book geeks. They know their trade and they know their stock and above all, they know their customers. So when one of their regulars who liked crime fiction came in and asked, "Anything new worth reading?" they were directed to my book. When the head of the local book club came in, the same thing happened with resultant sales of twenty copies. When tourists and passing trade came in, conversations were struck up, likes and dislikes discovered and if it fitted, my book was recommended.

The owners and I also kept in touch. Not regularly, but I would drop in every couple of months. They helped me understand book trade nuances and I kept them updated on the progress of my next novel. They offered to host the launch of it, (which they did in 2016) and still the sales kept coming.

In 2017, they invited me to join in with an event that they hosted for their readers. A ticketed event with nibbles and Champagne and me, alongside a mainstream children's author whose first book deal has gone global and another traditionally published author who has a pedigree of prestigious award wins behind her. Each of us are being treated on an equal footing, each valued by a bookstore that know their customers, know their books and know authors. Because of that, they do good business. In comparison, that first store in the same town couldn't get my penname correct when they contacted me.

So, Indie authors, seek out your Indie bookstores. Embrace them and garner a relationship with them, for you are your own publishing representative and bookshops that are staffed by book people, want to have that personal contact. So get in there, brave 'The Face' and get your book onto their shelves.

But of course, you may still need to get the word out a bit wider. That means the dreaded, marketing…

Marketing

It is fair to say that the ability to write should not be underestimated, nor should a good cover, or decent levels of editing, or a good price-point. All of these are important, but even if you have done all of that, should no one actually know that you have written a book, then it's probably fair to say no one is likely to buy it.

I mean you have the global reach through PoD. You can get to a worldwide audience of potential buyers through the online retailers (as well as your local bookshops as discussed) and what is more global than having your book available on Amazon? But, if you haven't heralded the release or even the existence of your book, who on earth is going to find it amongst the countless millions of other titles? Well, apart from you Mum, Dad, siblings, cousins, friends and passing strangers that you tell through face-to-face conversations.

Funnily enough, those conversations are your opening levels of marketing. Each conversation, each discussion about your book gets it into the world, or at least the knowledge of it into the world. All you need now is to talk to more and more and more people. Except that probably isn't the most ideal form of marketing. Not when you can make yourself a Twitter account, or Facebook page, perhaps an Instagram account. Then you can tell all and sundry about your book. Except, please don't.

Social Media

Social media is meant to be social.

I got this so wrong when I began. I mean seriously wrong. My Author's Facebook page pretty much consisted of me saying, over and over, "Look, I published a book! Look I published a book! Look I publ…" You get the idea.

Instead, what I should have been doing is engaging socially, sharing my pictures and stories that were nothing to do with my book directly. Every so often, I could then introduce something more directly related with writing and then, on the odd occasion, I could post a "Look I published a book…" without the risk of scaring everyone away or annoying them to the point where they ignored me. Like I said before, it was all new and there wasn't anyone to ask. Eventually I figured it out.

Marketing on social media can of course be backed up with taking out Facebook or Amazon adverts. Given how the Facebook algorithm changes on what seems a monthly basis the 'reach' of your posts, even to those who follow you on your page, gets less and less. Understandably the businesses behind the social platforms want you to pay if you want to get a commercial message about your book out. So, as more and more of the 'organic' reach dwindles, more and more will have to be paid for.

My company, Book Reality, was adamant that marketing had to be driven by the authors themselves and so we stated quite clearly that we *"didn't provide marketing services"* as it would be charging money for what would primarily be the author's own efforts.

However, after a few years and a lot of requests for "HELP", we finally looked into how we could best assist indy authors. A lot of research later and The Independent Authors Marketing (IAM) Program was our solution. It has three tiers, each aimed specifically to assist independent authors to raise their profile and that of their books both virtually and in the 'real world'. A lot of it is concerned with getting out into the world and making connections and contacts. To enable that, each author gets the services of a virtual assistant. The first tier is open to all and the 2nd and 3rd by request. To learn more about it you can visit here:

https://bookreality.com/mp/

Websites and Blogs and Competitions

So far then you have your face-to-face conversations and to that you added online social interactions. Perhaps it is time for you to have your own website and perhaps your own blog (Hmm... if like me you continually forget to update your blog then perhaps 'not so much'. But, don't do as I do in this instance... do as I recommend... Get a blog).

I would recommend that you spend a little to get a professional website made for you. It will probably save you in the long run. Although if you do go that way, make sure that once it is built you can update it and look after it yourself. You do NOT want to have to go back to a developer every time you need to change a page or a picture or a word. *(Yes our LAM program can offer that service too).*

Online is now looking quite good. But what about your local newspaper, radio station? Yes, yes and yes again. Reach out, make contact, be brazen. No one else is going to do it for you. *(Well, we will through LAM, but you get the gist – you can do this all yourself, or you can pay someone to help you, but ultimately someone has to do it. It won't occur miraculously).*

Engage with other writers. See if you can be interviewed online by other bloggers or podcasters. Enter your book into competitions which if you win will give you more opportunity for publicity, but BEWARE!!

There are some really shonky, very expensive competitions being run by not so well-known publishing entities, so check what is worth entering. A very good resource for this is the Alliance of Independent Authors website. They have conducted quite rigorous investigations into what is good value for the author and what is a money making machine for the organisers.

Above all, be creative and consistent with your marketing efforts. Think of it as a gently growing snowball that always requires its momentum to be maintained. One day it might turn into an avalanche driven by its own force, but mostly it will be you, on your own, pushing it along, often uphill.

Amazon's Author Central & A+ Content

Amazon do assist you a bit though. As well as their adverts you can and definitely should login to Amazon's Author Central, both in the US, the UK and the other country-specific sites including France, Germany, Japan and hopefully more as they become available.

This is a place for you to claim your titles, add a biography, photos, twitter feeds, videos and event notifications so that when someone clicks on your name in Amazon they find out about you.

Simply Google: Amazon Author Central for each of the countries, login and start making your profile. If you are not sure what to include, take a look at an author who already has a page linked from the main Amazon sites.

You also have access to Amazon A+ content where you can add images, text, and other information to your book page so as to engage readers and give them more enticements to buy your book.

Expert Marketing Courses and Freebies

There are also a vast array of courses run by many, many online 'gurus' who will teach you advanced marketing techniques including how to get the best from Facebook Ads, Amazon Marketing Services Ads, how to build up a mailing list of followers, how to reach out to readers near and far and how to become a best-selling author. I have no doubt whatsoever that some of these are worth every single penny you might spend on them and that they deliver on every single thing promised.

I also have no doubt that some of them aren't worth the time or the money you will expend on them. Which ones are which? I have no idea.

I haven't used any of them and I'm currently **not** sitting on my yacht out in the middle of the Caribbean Sea, so there you go. Proof that if you don't do their courses, you may not necessarily get rich.

I do know that in the early days I ran free giveaways of my eBooks to try and build up email lists and I did it using a program called InstaFreebie. That website and program worked well as a process, but at some point a couple of years ago I thought, "Hang on. Why am I giving this stuff away?"

Yes, I know the rationale behind it, if I give the first eBook in a series away for free then the reader, if they love it, will go and buy books two and three and all the rest. The thing is, in my experience, most didn't. I don't mean most didn't like my books, (yeah, I know some probably didn't) but I had great feedback and reviews from others, no, I mean that those people who took up the free eBook offers seemed to specialise in reading books like that. **Free books**. Giveaways. There were so many freebies out there they never had to buy another book in their life. All they had to do was fill up their Kindles or whatever, each week and read happily ever after. So I stopped. Want to read my books? Buy them.

eBook Marketing Mega Mailing Lists

Rather than giving my book away for nothing I started discounting it to an 'On Sale' price and began to use the eBook marketing companies that already have mass mailing lists and who will advertise your book to their subscribers for a fee.

From all the ones I have tried out I can recommend, EBooksoda, the Fussy Librarian, Pixelscroll, the Kindle Book

Review and of course, the biggest of them all and the Holy Grail of eBook advertising, BookBub.

Each do the same thing. Normally you will offer your eBook for a discounted price for a set period of a day or up to a week. The advertising company will send a picture of the cover, a description of the book and a link to where it can be bought to their subscribers. For a fee.

BookBub are the pinnacle of these companies as they have, quite literally, millions of subscribers. An advert that targets their US, Indian, Australian, Canadian and UK readers of Crime Fiction will go to 3million+ readers and can cost anything from $100 US dollars up to almost $4000. The returns are usually equally as impressive. However, everybody wants a BookBub deal and they accept only a few each day. I was turned down the first **twelve** times I applied. Eventually I was accepted and have enjoyed five more successful adverts with them. It is entirely due to BookBub that three of my books listed as Amazon category and general list bestsellers. Although it is not a silver bullet that is guaranteed.

The last advert I had with them ran on a weekday, I think I didn't discount the book price enough and it was during a holiday period when perhaps a lot of people who would otherwise have read the BookBub email were probably trying to wrangle their kids into some semblance of school holiday activity.

The sales were mediocre and the Return on Investment was negative. Saying that, on the one prior to that I made a few thousand dollars, so swings and roundabouts.

How do you register for any of these eBook marketing methods? Yeah, you guessed it. Go online and sign up with them. With regard to BookBub, make sure you Google BookBub Partner, as there is a reader login site as well. You don't want that, you want the author end of things.

Reader Reviews

One small word of caution on the BookBub phenomenon. Getting your book out to thousands of readers is great. Getting your book reviewed online by them is even better. However, not all reviews will be five-star and not all reviewers may, in fact, be sane. You have to take it on the chin.

When I got my first one-star review it twisted my very soul. Cut deep, hurt. I wanted to reply and berate this idiot who obviously had no concept of my talents. I wanted to. I didn't. Nor should you, ever. They have reviewed your book. They are entitled to their opinion. It would be lovely if they could be constructive. It would be lovely if they followed that old advice, "If you can't say anything nice, then don't say anything" but sadly the one-stars will be a burden you have to carry.

I get through it now by remembering there is a book on Amazon that has a one-star review which criticises it for being too slow and full of characters that are boring. I get through my angst by laughing about the fact that this particular one-star review was given to *Great Expectations* by Charles Dickens. So, if you get a one-star, you're in good company.

Finally, let's talk Festivals.

Festivals

Literary Festivals are not the exclusive hangout of traditionally published authors. Granted, it can be extremely difficult to get your foot in the door, or even your email replied to, but nothing is impossible. I went along to a smaller, local festival a few years ago that had decided to allow Indie authors a showcase opportunity. I had to pay for a table and a 'pitch' and I spent the weekend at the event selling a few books here and there. Most of the readers attending wanted to spend time with the internationally famous authors. I couldn't blame them, I did too.

Over the weekend I spoke to the Festival Director. I kept in touch. The following year they decided to have a panel on the phenomenon that is Indie. I was invited to take part. That attendance raised my profile. I met other festival authors and other festival directors. Since then I have attended four more festivals as a participant or host interviewer. This was not by some great strategy or design or because I am somehow 'gifted'. This was because I took a chance when that first opportunity was presented. It could have been a one-off, it could have been a waste of a couple of hundred dollars. As it was, it wasn't.

The Bottom Line

And really, that is the bottom line for marketing as an Indie author. Perhaps the bottom line for Indie authors in general.

No one will do your marketing, or anything else for you, just for fun. You have to do it yourself, or pay a reputable company to help you. There is no correct way of doing it, but there are many wrong ways (Most of which I did when I was starting out). Seek the opportunities and grasp them as best you can.

But be cheered. Those opportunities continue to grow. In 2022, the Miles Franklyn Award, Australia's most prestigious literature prize, shortlisted a self-published title. It didn't win, but that didn't matter. Cracks are appearing in the traditional publishing world. More awards will follow. More festivals will open to us. All you need remember is to promote yourself as a professional Indie author, be that in your on-line 'footprint' or in the face-to-face conversations with that person in the street who asks you, "What do you do?" Yes, you have to keep your spirits up when no one else is there to encourage you, but you will also enjoy the feelings and sensations of seeing your book published. Ultimately, it comes back to you answering that person in the street…

"What do I do? ...**I'm a writer.**"

Subscribe to our YouTube channel and Podcast by visiting:

https://linktr.ee/bookreality

Want to learn even more?

Train with the Book Reality Academy

E-Book Publishing

This comprehensive course will guide you through every step needed to successfully publish your eBook and see it for sale across the world's online bookstores.

Whether you're a new writer or an experienced one, this online course will provide you with the hands-on skills you need to be an independently published author.

What you will learn:

You'll learn what eBooks are, where they are sold and how royalties can be earned. You will be guided through, step-by-step, how to set-up your Kindle Direct Publishing account with Amazon, the biggest seller of eBooks in the world. We will show you exactly how to navigate the US tax registration system, so that you can reap the most royalty payments.

We will explain the pros and cons of Amazon's exclusive programs and to contrast and compare, you will also learn about aggregators. Not only how they work and how they help your book be sold in the widest marketplaces, but also how you set-up your account with, and upload your books to, one of the biggest of them, Draft2Digital.

Add to that, the hands-on skills to:

- Format your manuscript from a raw Microsoft® Word document into a ready-for-conversion file
- Use Calibre to convert those files
- Harness the power of Amazon's Kindle conversion process
- Use Draft2Digital and make your book available to online shops and libraries.

All of this, and much more, including a unit on promotion and marketing, is explained in the relaxed and fun manner that is the signature of a Book Reality Academy course.

This hands-on guide to eBook publishing is delivered in 'bite-size' training elements that can be squeezed into any coffee break, letting you learn at your own pace without tying you to your keyboard for days.

Your trainer:

Guiding you through the course in his relaxed and fun style is Ian Hooper, Executive Director of the Book Reality Experience, an Amazon best-selling Indy author in his own right and a trainer with over three decades of experience.

Don't miss out on this brilliant opportunity to take control of your online publications and become an author – it's no longer a dream, it's Your Book Reality.

https://book-reality-academy.thinkific.com/courses

Acknowledgements

I'd like to thank all those who have helped me to become an Indie author and whose encouragement and kindness have spurred me on through my journey.

Also, massive thanks to the consultants and contractors that work with us at The Book Reality Experience. The editors, illustrators, designers and marketing specialists who collectively help independent authors to make their mark in the world.

To the Festival Directors, award organisers and bookshop owners that have seen past the blinkers of the "traditional model" and embrace independent authors, thank you, may your influence continue to spread.

To the journalists and broadcasters, reviewers and critics who have interviewed, photographed and written favourably about me and other indies. Thanks. To the online reviewers who have given me terrible reviews, thanks anyway.

To every librarian I have ever met. They are Goddesses (and Gods) walking amongst us!

Especially a huge thank you to Ursula and Pauline for inaugurating the Skulduggery in Stowmarket festival, for always being approachable and for helping me with the logistics of the London Book Fair.

As usual though, my biggest thanks goes to my wife, Jacki, without whom, none of this happens.

About The Author

Ian Hooper was born in Northern Ireland in 1966. At eighteen he joined the Royal Air Force; originally training as an aircraft technician he was later commissioned as an Intelligence Officer. On leaving the Service he relocated to Western Australia and established a training consultancy.

His first novel, *A Time To Every Purpose*, an alternative history with a religious twist, was published independently in 2014 and gained positive critical acclaim.

His subsequent series of *Wright & Tran* detective novels has seen three released to date with the first, *Face Value*, receiving the New York based Publishers Weekly BookLife Prize for fiction in 2017. He also undertakes work as a ghost writer and has released a number of humorous poetry anthologies.

A passionate advocate of the Indie author scene, Ian initially ran training sessions for indy authors, before establishing the Book Reality Experience in 2015, a publishing assistance company that helps writers become independent authors.

In 2018 he established Leschenault Press, a small publisher that is (of course) independent.

Come visit us at:
www.bookreality.com

Email: create@bookreality.com

Absolutely Shameless
Advertising Opportunity

The Wright & Tran Novels

Face Value

When siblings Zoe and Michael Sterling insist that their middle-aged parents have gone missing, Kara and Tien are at first sceptical and then quickly intrigued; the father, ex-intelligence analyst Chris Sterling, appears to be involved with an elusive Russian thug.

Using less than orthodox methods and the services of ex-colleagues with highly specialised talents, Wright & Tran take on the case. But the truth they uncover is far from simple and will shake Zoe and Michael as much as it will challenge Tien and anger Kara. Anger she can ill afford for she is being hunted by others for the killing of a street predator who chose the wrong prey.

The only constant in this darkening world is that nothing and no one can be taken at face value.

"Two unusual private investigators with classified backgrounds take on a seemingly straightforward case to track down missing parents. With taut writing, bone-crushing action, and a pace that never relents, this was a difficult read to put down and a worthy winner."
Mark Dawson – New York Times Best Selling Author

Flight Path

Kara Wright and Tien Tran, combat veterans of an elite intelligence unit, now make their living as Private Investigators. Often working the mundane, just occasionally they get to use all their former training.

"I'd like you to make sure the dead are really dead."

So it is that the enigmatic Franklyn tasks Kara and Tien to investigate the apparent suicide of a local celebrity. Within days the women are embarked on a pursuit that leads halfway around the globe and into the darkest recesses of the human condition. Kara, Tien and their team will endure mental stress worse than anything they experienced from combat and, like combat, not everyone makes it home.

Fall Guys

"We want to know why the Brits are selling weapons to ISIS"

When a break-in threatens Britain's National Security, Franklyn calls on Wright & Tran but Kara will have to take this case on her own. Tien wants nothing to do with the world of Private Investigations and less to do with the world of Franklyn.

Kara goes solo, but finding who is responsible for the break-in is the easy part. Finding who the real criminals are is much, much harder.

Isolated in a world of half-truths and lies, international arms deals and power politics, she is quick to discover that she's been working for the wrong side. What she didn't figure on was that making amends will place her, and those she loves, in the sights of those who have everything to lose.

A Time To Every Purpose

What if Jesus hadn't been crucified?

For two thousand years humanity has been enveloped in Nirvana. But in the early decades of the 20th Century, natural disasters, famine, disease and economic collapse bring catastrophe and a fledgling Nazi Party sweeps to power. Now, almost a century later, their brutal persecution of millions is a never-ending holocaust.

Yet a few heroes remain.

Leigh Wilson, the preeminent scientist of her generation, has kept a secret all her life. But plunged into the aftermath of the cold-blooded murder of a Nazi official, she is forced to make a choice. Will she destroy what she loves to save what she can only imagine?

A Time to Every Purpose is a thrilling mix of science and action, good versus evil, and the eternal question all humans face: Is this my time to act?

"A Time To Every Purpose by Ian Andrew deals with huge concepts, looking at the broad sweep of history… a well-executed alternate history novel with some great action scenes."
John Wyatt, News UK

As Ian Hooper

The Little Book Of Silly Rhymes & Odd Verses

An illustrated collection of humorous, daft, sometimes sad and occasionally thought provoking verses. Illustrations by Alison Mutton.

Slaughtered Nursery Rhymes

An unlucky for some collection of 13 Nursery Rhymes for all the adults who want to know what really happened to Jack and Jill, Little Bo Peep and Doctor Foster. Not to mention what Mary was actually growing in her garden!

When we think of a rhyme, with which we passed time, as a child in the playground at school,
It would be a short ditty, but much more the pity, it'd be quite mundane as a rule.
For old Jack and Miss Jill, would never speak ill, of their partner beside them in verse.
But it caused me to wonder, if the truth we could plunder, would their actual behaviour be worse?
Would we discover, that Jill was a lover, of violence and mayhem and death?
Or would Little Bo Peep, being fed up with sheep, curse them silently under her breath?
And so in this book, we'll be taking a look at the criminal lives of a few,
Of our favourite "rhymees", and I trust it will please, or at least raise a giggle or two!

Index

A

Aggregator, 14, 15, 19, 20, 22, 39, 42, 43
Amazon
    ACX, 22, 104, 107
    KDP, 15, 16, 17, 18, 19, 20, 21, 24, 25, 27, 28, 29, 30, 33, 34, 36, 37, 38, 39, 40, 41, 42, 45, 46, 47, 49, 50, 53, 54, 56, 57, 58, 59, 60, 62, 63, 64, 65, 68, 70, 73, 74, 75, 76, 79, 83, 84, 88, 91, 97, 99, 102, 109, 110, 114

D

Draft2Digital, 14, 15, 19, 20, 22, 38, 39, 40, 43, 44, 45, 46, 47, 48, 49, 50, 68, 70, 84, 86, 99, 100, 101, 102, 104, 109, 110

E

Expanded Distribution, 17, 18, 56, 62, 63

F

Festivals, 124, 125
Findaway Voices, 15, 22, 104, 109, 110
Format
    Audio Book, 8, 13, 15, 19, 22, 23, 38, 103, 104, 105, 106, 109, 110, 111
    eBook, 13, 15, 16, 24, 30, 31, 33, 35, 36, 37, 39, 40, 41, 45, 46, 47, 49, 50, 51, 57, 68, 72, 84, 85, 86, 87, 88, 89, 90, 91, 92, 96, 99, 100, 102, 110, 122, 123
    Hardback, 11, 13, 17, 30, 38, 52, 53, 72, 74, 76, 85, 90
    Paperback, 13, 17, 19, 30, 31, 33, 38, 53, 54, 57, 60, 62, 64, 66, 72, 73, 74, 76, 77, 84, 85, 90

I

ISBN, 18, 37, 38, 39, 47, 55, 63, 71, 73, 74, 101, 110

L

Libraries, 18, 39, 49, 50, 52, 60, 79, 110, 112, 113, 114
Legal Deposit, 112, 113

M

Marketing, 4, 6, 25, 35, 41, 43, 117, 118, 119, 120, 121, 122, 123, 125
Microsoft®, 20, 35, 85, 86, 92
Word®, 36, 85, 86, 92

P

Publisher's Imprint, 37, 58, 73, 101

R

Returns Mechanism, 15, 77, 114, 123

T

Trim Size, 52, 53, 55, 58, 63, 66, 67, 73, 74, 75, 76, 87, 88, 89

For your notes

Leschenault Press

www.ingramcontent.com/pod-product-compliance
Lightning Source LLC
Chambersburg PA
CBHW050246120526
44590CB00016B/2233